AMERICAN UNIVERSITY

NATIONAL SECURITY LAW BRIEF

THE FORUM ON NATIONAL SECURITY LAW

Volume IX • Supplement • Number 1 • Summer 2018

American University Washington College of Law
Washington, DC

NATIONAL SECURITY LAW BRIEF

The Forum on National Security Law, Volume IX, Supplement, Number 1 (Summer 2018)

ISBN-13: 978-1090328854
ISBN-10: 1090328850

ISSN: 2160-102X

Founded in April 2009, the *American University National Security Law Brief* is the nation's first student-run law school publication to focus on the rapidly evolving field of national security law. The publication is published twice a year, with a complementary online component, and is edited and published by students at American University Washington College of Law.

The views and opinions expressed in the articles are solely those of the respective authors and do not necessarily represent those of the authors' employers, the publication, the editorial board, American University, or Washington College of Law

The Brief welcomes manuscript submissions on relevant topics in national security law and policy

For more information about the publication, submissions, or permissions, please visit the brief's website

Website: nationalsecuritylawbrief.com
Twitter: @AUNatlSecLa
Facebook: @AUNatlSecLaw
LinkedIn: linkedin.com/company/AUNatlSecLaw

Bluebook abbreviation: AM. U. NAT'L SEC. L. BRIEF F.

American University National Security Law Brief
Washington College of Law
American University
4300 Nebraska Avenue NW
Washington, DC 20016

Cover and design by Kevin D. Reyes (consulting editor) (kevindreyes.com)
Printed by CreateSpace, an Amazon Company

AMERICAN UNIVERSITY

NATIONAL SECURITY LAW BRIEF
THE FORUM ON NATIONAL SECURITY LAW

Volume IX • Supplement • Number I • Summer 2018

Contents

Editorial Note

Dear Readers,

This issue is the inaugural issue of *The Forum on National Security Law*. It was one of the goals of the past executive board to expand into the realm of electronic publications, and we are very excited to finally bring it to fruition! That said, within these pages, you will find a range of topics on national security law, including a bibliographic overview of the Fourth Amendment as it relates to national security, the issue of arming recreational drones, digital encryption, and the tension between border security and international relations.

Eight years ago, our founding counterparts set their intentions and academic convictions to paper in the enclosed blog post. In establishing this Brief, those who came before us threw down a gauntlet, calling upon law students to come together to enhance and underline essential debates in the National Security realm, anchoring them in legal analysis. This is a gauntlet we, the editorial board for Volume IX of the National Security Law Brief, gladly pick up. In the years since the Brief published its first issue, the world has changed immeasurably. Over the existence of the Brief, our staffers have seen the rise of ISIL; the fall of long-standing regimes in Egypt, Libya and Tunisia; and the re-solidification of old Cold War battle lines. What the next nine, nineteen or ninety years hold for the national security field is uncertain. What is certain, however, is that learned debate and discussion on critical topics requires an outlet, and that is what this publication strives to provide.

Very Respectfully,

Prescott A. Heighton
Editor-in-Chief

THE FORUM ON NATIONAL SECURITY LAW: A PUBLICATION OF THE AMERICAN UNIVERSITY NATIONAL SECURITY LAW BRIEF, vol. IX, supplement, no. 1 (Summer 2018), pp. 1–2.

THE FOURTH AMENDMENT, NATIONAL SECURITY, AND TERRORISM: A BIBLIOGRAPHIC ESSAY

*By Brent E. Newton**

INTRODUCTION

Perhaps the most difficult and compelling issue arising under the Fourth Amendment is how it is applied in the contexts of terrorism and national security. That difficulty is the result of the clash of two of the most powerful forces in law, liberty and the need for security. As much or more than any other provision in the Bill of Rights, the Fourth Amendment's protections—the specific "warrant" requirement and related "probable cause" requirement, as well as the general "reasonableness" requirement[1]—were designed to protect people's liberty regarding both their privacy and property.[2] Those protections apply to both innocent people as well as dangerous criminals who have committed the most serious of offenses.[3] Yet, except during outright wartime,[4] our society's fundamental

---

* The author is Deputy Staff Director of the United States Sentencing Commission and also serves as an adjunct professor of law at American University Washington College of Law and Georgetown University Law Center, where he teaches Criminal Procedure. The views expressed in this essay are the author's alone and do not reflect the position of the Commission.

[1] *See* Russell W. Galloway, *Basic Fourth Amendment Analysis*, 32 SANTA CLARA R. REV. 737, 748-78 (1992) (discussing the "warrant," "probable cause," and "reasonableness" requirements of the Fourth Amendment).

[2] *See, e.g.,* Riley v. California, 134 S. Ct. 2473, 2484-85, 2488-89, 2491, 2493 (2014) (discussing privacy interests protected by the Fourth Amendment in the context of searches of cellphones at the U.S. Border); Jardines v. Florida, 133 S. Ct. 1409, 1414-15, 1417 (2013) (discussing property interests protected by the Fourth Amendment in the context of a dog sniffing case).

[3] *See, e.g.,* Payton v. New York, 445 U.S. 573, 602 (1980) (finding violation of Fourth Amendment and suppressing evidence used to convict the defendant of murder).

[4] Some advocates for exempting Fourth Amendment protections for suspected terrorists contend that antiterrorism measures involving warrantless searches and seizures are justified under traditional military powers (which are not subject to the Fourth Amendment). *See, e.g.,* Memorandum of John C. Yoo to Alberto Gonzalez, at 25 (October 23, 2001),

security—security in people's bodies and property and, to a greater extent, national security—has never been more threatened than it has been from modern terrorism, whether international or domestic.[5]

Balancing liberty and security in the context of searches and seizures seeking to deter, detect, and prevent terrorism has been a challenge for courts in two primary contexts. First, both before and after Congress enacted the Foreign Intelligence Surveillance Act of 1978 (FISA)[6] and subsequent amendments to FISA,[7] courts have grappled with the constitutionality of "wiretaps" and other methods of monitoring communications of suspected terrorists and others who may threaten national security.[8] Second, courts have been required to assess physical seizures and searches of persons and their property—

---

https://www.justice.gov/sites/default/files/opa/legacy/2009/03/09/memomilit aryforcecombatus10232001.pdf (contending that "the Fourth Amendment does *not* apply to domestic military operations designed to deter and prevent further terrorist attacks"); *see also* Debra Cassens Weiss, *DOJ Endorsed Terrorism Exception to 4th Amendment in Another Disavowed Memo*, ABA JOURNAL (Apr. 4, 2008), http://abajournal.com/news/article/doj_endorsed_ terrorism_exception_to_4th_amendment_in_another_disavowed_memo/.

[5] *See, e.g.*, N. R. Kleinfield, *U.S. Attacked: Hijacked Jets Destroy Twin Towers and Hit Pentagon in Day of Terror*, N.Y. TIMES (Sept. 12, 2001), https://nytimes.com/2001/09/12/us/us-attacked-hijacked-jets-destroy-twin-towers-and-hit-pentagon-in-day-of-terror.html; David Johnston, *At Least 31 Are Dead and Scores Are Missing After Car Bomb Attack in Oklahoma City Wrecks 9-Story Federal Office Building*, N.Y. TIMES (Apr. 20, 1995), https://archive.nytimes.com/www.nytimes.com/learning/general/onthisday/ big/0419.html?scp=1&sq=At%2520Least%252031%2520Are%2520Dead,%252 0Scores%2520Are%2520Missing%2520After%2520Car%2520Bomb%2520Atta ck%2520in%2520Oklahoma%2520City%2520Wrecks%25209-Story%2520Federal%2520Office%2520Building&st=cse.

[6] Pub. L. No. 95-511, 92 Stat. 1783 (1978).

[7] FISA has been amended significantly since 1978. *See, e.g.*, FISA Amendments Act of 2008, Pub. L. No. 110-261, 122 Stat. 2465 (2008); USA PATRIOT Act, Pub. L. No. 107-56, 115 Stat. 1402 (2001).

[8] *See, e.g.*, ACLU v. NSA, 438 F. Supp. 2d 754 (E.D. Mich. 2006), *rev'd*, 493 F.3d 644 (6th Cir. 2007) (2-1 decision), *cert. denied*, 552 U.S. 1179 (2008) (concerning persons who conducted regular international communications and believed the National Security Agency's (NSA) secret program for warrantless interception of international telephone and internet communications violated their Fourth Amendment rights).

usually in the context of warrantless seizures and searches in public venues or on public transportation—intended to deter potential terrorists and uncover instrumentalities of terrorism, such as weapons of mass destruction.[9] The cases decided to date, a handful of Supreme Court cases (some only briefing addressing the issue in passing dicta) and many lower court decisions, have generated a significant amount of legal scholarship about the Fourth Amendment, national security, and terrorism.[10] Many important legal issues remain unresolved, however.[11]

This succinct bibliographic essay addresses Fourth Amendment issues in both contexts. It provides citations to, and brief summaries of, both the leading cases and the leading works of relevant legal scholarship. Finally, this essay also addresses two specific issues that recur in discussions about the Fourth Amendment and terrorism: the threshold issue of what constitutes "terrorism" (so as to justify possible special treatment under the Fourth Amendment); and the question of whether the Constitution permits the race, ethnicity, or religion of a suspected terrorist to factor into the legal analysis of whether there was a valid basis to search or seize that person.

The bibliography set forth below, while not exhaustive, is comprehensive. It is intended to assist both academics as well as judges and practitioners in their research of these difficult Fourth Amendment issues. It also offers primary and secondary sources around which an upper-level course or seminar at a law school could be structured.

I.   MONITORING THE COMMUNICATIONS OF SUSPECTED TERRORISTS

Law enforcement officers' electronic monitoring of criminal suspects' communications began shortly after the telephone became

---

[9] *See, e.g.,* MacWade v. Kelly, 460 F.3d 260 (2d Cir. 2006) (concerning a Fourth Amendment challenge to New York Police Department's random, suspicionless searches of baggage for explosives and weapons as the owners were entering the New York City subway system).

[10] *See, infra* Section III.

[11] For instance, the Supreme Court has never directly addressed the constitutionality of either FISA or an anti-terrorism preventative search of members of the public in contexts such as mass transportation or sporting events.

commonplace in the beginning of the twentieth century.[12] The Supreme Court originally concluded that the Fourth Amendment offered suspects no protection from such monitoring so long as law enforcement did not physically trespass on a suspect's property through the installation of a wiretap or other remote listening devices.[13] By the 1950s and 1960s, during the Cold War, warrantless wiretapping and bugging of suspected communist spies became extremely common.[14]

In 1967, in *Katz v. United States*,[15] the Supreme Court dramatically changed the course of its Fourth Amendment jurisprudence by holding that electronic monitoring of criminal suspects was a "search" under the Fourth Amendment if the person being monitored had *a reasonable expectation of privacy* in his or her conversation, thus applying both the warrant and probable cause requirements to such monitoring.[16] In footnote 23 to the Court's opinion, however, the Court noted its holding was not necessarily applicable to electronic monitoring for national security purposes.[17] Five years later, in *United*

---

[12] *See, e.g.,* Olmstead v. Unites States, 277 U.S. 438 (1928) (addressing constitutionality of a warrantless wiretap of defendant's home telephone).

[13] *See id.* at 465-66 (1928) (holding that law enforcement officers' warrantless use of a wiretap did not violate the Fourth Amendment because the officers did not physically trespass on the defendant's property); *see also* Goldman v. United States, 316 U.S. 129, 134-36 (1940) (holding that law enforcement officers' use of an electronic listening device, a "bug," did not violate the defendant's Fourth Amendment right because the officers did not physically trespass on the defendant's property).

[14] *See* L. Rush Atkinson, *The Fourth Amendment's National Security Exception: Its History and Limits,* 66 VAND. L. REV. 1343, 1365-67, 1371-72 (2013).

[15] 389 U.S. 347 (1967).

[16] *Id.* at 351-52, 359.

[17] *Id.* at 358 n.23 (1967) ("Whether safeguards other than prior authorization by a magistrate would satisfy the Fourth Amendment in a situation involving the national security is a question not presented by this case."); *see also id.* at 363 (White, J., concurring) ("In joining the Court's opinion, I note the Court's acknowledgement that there are circumstances in which it is reasonable to search without a warrant. In this connection, in footnote 23 the Court points out that today's decision does not reach national security cases. Wiretapping to protect the Nation has been authorized by successive Presidents. The present Administration would apparently save national security cases from restrictions against wiretapping.").

States v. United States District Court (Keith),[18] the Court extended *Katz* to electronic monitoring of suspects' communications concerning *domestic* threats to national security but left open the question of whether the Fourth Amendment permitted warrantless monitoring concerning threats to national security by *foreign* persons or their agents within the United States.[19]

In 1978, Congress entered the fray by enacting FISA, which created a special court system, the Foreign Intelligence Surveillance Court (FISC), subject to appellate review by a special appellate panel and, ultimately, by the Supreme Court.[20] Among other things, FISA created a special warrant application process, requiring probable cause to believe that "the target of the electronic surveillance is a foreign power" (including an international terrorist organization rather than a government)[21] or "an agent of a foreign power" (including a U.S. citizen agent)[22] and that the surveillance will yield "foreign intelligence information."[23] The court does *not*, however, require probable cause that the person or persons being monitored are breaking the law in some manner that threatens national security or

---

[18] 407 U.S. 297 (1972).

[19] *Id.* at 308-09 (noting "the instant case requires no judgment on the scope of the President's surveillance power with respect to the activities of foreign powers, within or without this country" because the warrantless wiretaps in the instant case were done "to protect the nation from attempts of domestic organizations to attack and subvert the existing structure of Government"); *see also id.* at 322-23 ("Different standards may be compatible with the Fourth Amendment if they are reasonable both in relation to the legitimate need of Government for intelligence information and the protected rights of our citizens.").

[20] *See* 50 U.S.C. § 1803 (2018).

[21] *See* 50 U.S.C. § 1801(a)(4) (2018) (defining "foreign power" to include "a group engaged in international terrorism or activities in preparation therefor").

[22] If the target is a "United States person" (a U.S. citizen or permanent resident), FISA requires a showing that the information sought "cannot be reasonably obtained by normal investigative techniques," 50 U.S.C. § 1804(a)(6)(E) (2018), "the information sought is the type of foreign intelligence information designated," *id.*, and "the certification or certifications are not clearly erroneous." 50 U.S.C. § 1805(a)(4) (2018).

[23] *See* 50 U.S.C. § 1805 (2018).

constitutes terrorism.[24] Notably, an "agent of a foreign power"[25] may include a suspected so-called "lone wolf" terrorist with no direct link to a foreign government or international terrorist organization but who acts with the intent to promote the terrorist goals of a foreign power or international terrorist organization.[26] Evidence of crime (including terrorism and national security offenses) uncovered during surveillance authorized by FISA may be used in a criminal prosecution[27] and is not subject to suppression under the Fourth Amendment's exclusionary rule.[28] In addition to having engaged in surveillance pursuant to FISA, the federal government at different times—both before and after FISA—has engaged in warrantless surveillance of suspected terrorists and persons posing threats to national security, both within and outside the country.[29]

---

[24] *See* 50 U.S.C. §§ 1804(a)(3), 1804(a)(6), 1805 (2018) (indicating only that the Government needs to *believe* that the target is a foreign power or acting as an agent of a foreign power).

[25] 50 U.S.C. § 1801(b) (2018).

[26] *See* 50 U.S.C. § 1801(b)(1)(C), § 1801(b)(2)(C) (2018).

[27] *See* 50 U.S. Code § 1806(b) (2018).

[28] *See, e.g.,* United States v. Mahamud, 838 F. Supp. 2d 881, 888 (D. Minn. 2012) (agreeing with precedent in declining to suppress evidence uncovered by FISA surveillance on the grounds that FISA has an arguably lower probable cause standard than that required by the Fourth Amendment).

[29] *See, e.g., Katz v. United States,* 389 U.S. 347, 363 (1967) (White, J., concurring) ("Wiretapping [without a judicial warrant] to protect the Nation has been authorized by successive Presidents. The present Administration would apparently save national security cases from restrictions against wiretapping."); Tracey Maclina, *The Bush Administration's Terrorist Surveillance Program and the Fourth Amendment Warrant Requirement: Lessons from Justice Powell and the Keith Case,* 41 U.C. DAVIS L. REV. 1259, 1293 (2008) ("In the weeks following the September 11, 2001 terrorist attacks, President Bush authorized the NSA to initiate the [Terrorist Surveillance Program or] TSP. While the precise details of the TSP remain confidential, the government has acknowledged that, as originally implemented, the program involves electronic surveillance without judicial approval. Specifically, the TSP covers 'telephone and email communications where one party to the communication is located outside the United States and the NSA has a reasonable basis to conclude that one party to the communication is a member of al Qaeda, affiliated with al Qaeda, or a member of an organization affiliated with al Qaeda, or working in support of al Qaeda.'").

The following cases and scholarly works have addressed a variety of Fourth Amendment issues related to monitoring of communications or movements of suspected terrorists or persons threatening national security.

A. Selected Case Law

Carpenter v. United States.[30] The Court held that probable cause and a search warrant are ordinarily required for law enforcement officers to obtain historical cell-tower records showing the movement of a suspect's cell phone for a period of seven days or more.[31] Towards the end of its opinion, the Court observed that "[o]ur decision today is a narrow one. . . . [O]ur opinion does not consider other collection techniques involving foreign affairs or national security."[32] The Court also noted that the "exigent circumstances" exception to the warrant requirement could permit officers to obtain historical cell-tower records without a warrant to prevent a "bomb" threat.[33]

United States v. Jones.[34] Although the majority opinion did not address the issue, a four-Justice concurrence stated, after contending that long-term warrantless GPS monitoring of a drug dealer's automobile violated the defendant's reasonable expectation of privacy in violation of the Fourth Amendment, "[w]e . . . need not consider whether prolonged GPS monitoring in the context of investigations involving extraordinary offenses [such as terrorism] would . . . intrude on a constitutionally protected sphere of privacy in the same manner that it would for ordinary criminal offenses."[35] In *Carpenter,* a majority of the Court adopted the *Jones* concurring opinions' rationale in the context of historical cell tower records, yet the Court's holding seems fully applicable to GPS records as well.[36]

---

[30] 138 S.Ct. 2206, 2221 (2018).

[31] *Id.* at 2221 (holding that, generally speaking, police needed to obtain a warrant for extensive historic cell-site records collection).

[32] *Id.* at 2220.

[33] *Id.* at 2220-23.

[34] 565 U.S. 400 (2012).

[35] *Id.* at 431 (Alito, J., concurring).

[36] *See Carpenter*, 138 S.Ct. at 2215, 2217.

Wikimedia Foundation v. NSA.[37] Educational, legal, human rights, and media organizations filed a lawsuit seeking declaratory and injunctive relief against National Security Agency, alleging that NSA's interception, collection, review, and storing of organizations' international text-based communications, through NSA's "Upstream" surveillance program pursuant to section 702 of FISA, violated the Fourth Amendments and exceeded NSA's authority under FISA.[38] The district court held that all of the plaintiffs lacked standing, but the Fourth Circuit concluded that the media organization plaintiff plausibly alleged that NSA was intercepting and copying some of its international text-based communications, which provided standing to raise the Fourth Amendment claim.[39] The Fourth Circuit distinguished the Supreme Court's decision in *Clapper v. Amnesty International USA*[40] in which the Court had found that the plaintiffs, in that case, lacked standing to challenge NSA's surveillance program because they had not offered evidence that NSA was monitoring their communications.[41] The Fourth Circuit held that the other plaintiffs in *Wikimedia* lacked standing, however, because they had not provided sufficient proof that their communications were being monitored.[42] Judge Davis concurred in part and dissented in part, contending that the other plaintiffs possessed standing to raise their Fourth Amendment claims.[43]

---

[37] 857 F.3d 193 (4th Cir. 2016)

[38] *Id.* at 202.

[39] *Id.* at 200.

[40] 568 U.S. 398 (2013) (denying that a group of labor, legal and media organizations had standing to bring suits related to foreign intelligence surveillance on the basis of the failure to demonstrate future injury was imminent and that the alleged future injury was sufficiently related to the FISA Act provision at issue).

[41] *Id.* at 401-02.

[42] 857 F. 3d at 207-08.

[43] *Id.* at 217 (Davis, J., concurring) (specifically delineating that while Wikimedia itself did not have sufficient standing, the non-Wikimedia plaintiffs could have had standing, a list which included the organizations Human Rights Watch, The Rutherford Institute, Washington Office on Latin America, Amnesty International, and the National Association of Criminal Defense Attorneys).

United States v. Mohamud.[44] The Ninth Circuit affirmed the district court's denial of the defendant's motion to suppress evidence of his email communications with a foreign national in which the defendant expressed his intent to engage in terrorist acts in the United States.[45] The defendant challenged the warrantless search of the foreign national's e-mails under section 702 of FISA—which incidentally revealed the defendant's email communications with the foreign national—but the district court and Ninth Circuit concluded that the warrantless search was reasonable under the Fourth Amendment.[46] The search was done to protect the United States from a "terrorist threat and did not stray into the broader category of the conduct of foreign affairs," and the government employed reasonable targeting and minimization procedures.[47]

Klyman v. Obama.[48] The district court granted a preliminary injunction after finding a likelihood that the plaintiffs would succeed in their claim that section 215 of FISA—which permits the federal government to collect bulk telephonic and internet metadata from commercial communication services (but not information about the content of such communications), including metadata about the domestic communications of U.S. citizens—violated the Fourth Amendment.[49] The D.C. Circuit vacated the judgment of the district court on the threshold ground that the plaintiffs appeared to lack standing to raise their Fourth Amendment claim.[50] The decision of the

---

[44] 843 F.3d 420 (9th Cir. 2016).

[45] *Id.* at 423-24.

[46] *Id.* at 431. *See* Orin Kerr, *The Surprisingly Weak Reasoning of Mohamud*, LAWFARE, (Dec. 23, 2016) https://www.lawfareblog.com/surprisingly-weak-reasoning-mohamud (examining the reasoning in Mahmoud and examining the role of the term "incidental").

[47] *Mohamud*, 843 F.3d at 441-42 (holding that because the conduct did not extend further than trying to prevent terrorist operations, the court need not determine whether the collection of foreign affairs communications is reasonable as a categorical matter).

[48] 957 F. Supp. 2d 1 (D. D.C. 2013), *vacated and remanded*, 800 F.3d 559 (D.C. Cir. 2015) (per curiam).

[49] 957 F. Supp. 2d at 10.

[50] 800 F.3d at 561 (reversing the decision of the district court and remanding for further proceedings for reasons explained in the opinions of Brown, J. and Williams, J. respecting the decision).

court on this issue was divided, with Judge Brown writing separately to emphasize the importance of secrecy to the proper function of our government institutions.[51]

Redacted Order.[52] This case is a rare example of a publicly released (albeit redacted) order from the Foreign Intelligence Surveillance Court denying (in part) a FISA application related to upstream collections on Fourth Amendment grounds.[53] The court determined that the NSA's targeting procedures were not "reasonably designed" to minimize collection and retention of date from unconsenting United States persons, and was unable to determine that the targeting and minimizations procedures were consistent with the Fourth Amendment.[54]

In Re Directives.[55] The Foreign Intelligence Surveillance Review Court held that the Protect America Act of 2007 (PAA),[56] which amended FISA by allowing the federal government to conduct warrantless surveillance of targets (including U.S. citizens) reasonably believed to be outside of the United States, did not violate the Fourth Amendment.[57] The court specifically upheld the PAA under a "foreign intelligence exception" to the Fourth Amendment, a species of the Fourth Amendment "special needs" doctrine.[58] Recognizing that the government's interest in protecting national security is "intense," the court held that such an interest outweighed any privacy interest of those outside the U.S. being monitored.[59]

Mayfield v. United States.[60] In this civil rights action, the district court held that the PATRIOT Act, which amended FISA by allowing

---

[51] *Id.* at 565-66.

[52] 2011 WL 10945618 (F.I.S.C. Oct. 3, 2011).

[53] *Id.* at *1.

[54] *Id.* at *9.

[55] 551 F.3d 1004 (F.I.S. Rev. Ct. 2008).

[56] Pub. L. No. 110-55, 121 Stat. 552 (2007).

[57] 551 F.3d at 1007.

[58] *Id.* at 1010 (affirming the decision of the FISC on its understanding of the Fourth Amendment Warrant Clause's Foreign Intelligence Exception, over the arguments of the petitioner that such an exception did not exist); *Id.* at 1011 (applying "special needs" precedent to determine that the foreign intelligence exception was legitimate in this case).

[59] *Id.* at 1011.

[60] 504 F. Supp. 2d 1023 (D. Ore. 2007), *vacated*, 599 F.3d 964 (9th Cir. 2010).

for surveillance of foreign powers or their agents so long as a "substantial" purpose (even if not the "primary" purpose) was to monitor foreign powers or their agents, violated the Fourth Amendment. On appeal, the Ninth Circuit vacated the judgment of the district court after concluding that the plaintiff did not possess Article III standing to litigate the Fourth Amendment claim.[61]

ACLU v. NSA.[62] In this civil rights action, the district court invalidated the George W. Bush Administration's Terrorist Surveillance Program (TPS) as violating the Fourth Amendment.[63] The Sixth Circuit, in a 2-1 decision, reversed the district court's injunction against the TSP after concluding that the plaintiffs lacked standing under Article III to raise the Fourth Amendment claim.[64]

In Re Sealed Case.[65] The Foreign Intelligence Surveillance Court of Review upheld the amendments to FISA by the Patriot Act of 2001 in the first recorded case to be appealed to the Court of Review.[66] In particular, the court held that permitting the government to conduct surveillance of agents of foreign powers, if foreign intelligence is a "significant" (as opposed to the "primary") purpose of such surveillance, does not violate Fourth Amendment.[67]

United States v. Bin Laden.[68] The district court held that there is a "foreign intelligence collection" exception to the Fourth Amendment that applied to a warrantless search of a U.S. citizen's home in a foreign country that was authorized by the President or Attorney General.[69] The court further held that a warrantless wiretap of the same U.S. citizen's telephone abroad was done without the authorization of the President or Attorney General and, thus, violated

---

[61] 599 F.3d at 965.

[62] 438 F. Supp. 2d 754, 773-75 (E.D. Mich. 2006), *rev'd*, 493 F.3d 644, 673-74 (6th Cir. 2007).

[63] 438 F. Supp. 2d at 782 (holding additionally that the program violated Separation of Powers doctrine, the Administrative Procedures Act (Pub. L. No. 79-404, 60 Stat. 237 (1946)) and the First Amendment).

[64] 493 F.3d at 648.

[65] 310 F.3d 717 (F.I.S. Rev. Ct. 2002) (per curiam).

[66] *Id.* at 719-20.

[67] *Id.* at 723.

[68] 126 F. Supp.2d 264 (S.D.N.Y. 2000), *aff'd*, *In re Terrorist Bombings of U.S. Embassies in East Africa*, 552 F.3d 157 (2d Cir. 2008).

[69] 126 F. Supp. 2d at 271-72.

the Fourth Amendment.[70] However, the court refused to apply the Fourth Amendment's exclusionary rule to the evidence obtained during that warrantless search.[71] On appeal, the Second Circuit held more generally that the Fourth Amendment warrant requirement does not apply to searches abroad, even searches of U.S. citizens.[72] The Second Circuit nevertheless held that the general Fourth Amendment "reasonableness" requirement does apply to such searches and that the warrantless searches, in this case, were reasonable.[73]

United States v. Pelton.[74] The Fourth Circuit rejected a Fourth Amendment challenge to FISA and also held that incriminating evidence properly uncovered during surveillance authorized by FISA is admissible in a criminal prosecution.[75]

United States v. Duggan.[76] In a federal criminal prosecution of members of the Irish Republican Army based on evidence obtained during a wiretap authorized by the FISC, the Second Circuit upheld FISA as adequately balancing the defendants' Fourth Amendment rights against the federal government's strong interest in protecting national security.[77]

United States v. Truong Dinh Hung.[78] In a case in which the government engaged in warrantless surveillance before the effective date of FISA, the Fourth Circuit recognized a "foreign intelligence exception" to the Fourth Amendment, and permitted the evidence obtained during such warrantless surveillance to be admitted in a criminal prosecution.[79]

---

[70] *Id.* at 280-81.

[71] *Id.* at 284.

[72] 552 F.3d at 167 (discussing the extraterritorial applicability of the Fourth Amendment Warrant Requirement).

[73] *Id.*

[74] 835 F.2d 1067 (4th Cir. 1987).

[75] *Id.* at 1069; *id.* at 1076 (concurring with the decision of the Second Circuit in *United States v. Duggan* (*infra* note 74)).

[76] 743 F.2d 59 (2d Cir. 1984).

[77] *Id.* at 64-65 (affirming the convictions of the defendants).

[78] 629 F.2d 908 (4th Cir. 1980).

[79] *Id.* at 911-12.

Zweibon v. Mitchell.[80] In a divided en banc decision that failed to garner a majority of the eight judges in any one opinion, the plurality opinion concluded that a search warrant is required before a wiretap is installed on a domestic organization that is neither the agent of nor acting in collaboration with, a foreign power. The plurality concluded that this is so even if the surveillance was directed by the President in the name of foreign intelligence gathering for protection of the national security.[81]

B. Leading Legal Scholarship[82]

L. Rush Atkinson, *The Fourth Amendment's National Security Exception: Its History and Limits.*[83] Atkinson traces the history of the "pure intelligence rule" — the federal executive branch's traditional use of warrantless surveillance solely for the purposes of national security and anti-terrorism, with the corresponding policy of not using the evidentiary fruits of such surveillance in criminal prosecutions.[84] Based on that tradition of "self-restraint" in use such evidence in criminal prosecutions, Atkinson contends that such warrantless surveillance is reasonable under the "special needs" exception to the Fourth Amendment because it is not primarily for law enforcement purposes.[85]

---

[80] 516 F.2d 594 (D.C. Cir. 1975) (en banc).

[81] *Id.* at 600-01.

[82] *See also* Matthew A. Anzaldi; Jonathan W. Gannon, *In Re Directives Pursuant to Section 105B of the Foreign Intelligence Surveillance Act: Judicial Recognition of Certain Warrantless Foreign Intelligence Surveillance,* 88 TEX. L. REV. 1599, 1632 (2010); Geoffrey S. Corn, *Encryptions, Asymmetric Warfare, and the Need for Lawful Access,* 26 WM. & MARY BILL RTS. J. 337, 360 (2017); Jeffrey Kahn, *The Unreasonable Rise of Reasonable Suspicion: Terrorist Watchlists and Terry v. Ohio,* 26 WM. & MARY BILL RTS. J. 383, 406 (2017); Orin S. Kerr, *The Modest Role of the Warrant Clause in National Security Investigations,* 88 TEX. L. REV. 1669, 1684 (2010); Caren Morrison, *Private Actors, Corporate Data and National Security: What Assistance Do Tech Companies Owe Law Enforcement,* 26 WM. & MARY BILL RTS. J. 407, 436 (2017).

[83] 66 VAND. L. REV. 1343 (2013).

[84] *Id.* at 1357-59.

[85] *Id.* at 1390-92.

William C. Banks, *The Death of FISA*.[86] Banks traces the history of electronic surveillance of persons suspected of national security and terrorism offenses before and after FISA, including after the 9/11 terrorist attacks.[87] He contends that FISA is in some ways outmoded based on unforeseeable developments in technology and international terrorism and requires significant revision to remain both effective and constitutional in the future.[88]

Emily Berman, *Quasi-Constitutional Protections and Government Surveillance*.[89] Berman's article offers a defense of criticisms of the FISC and contends that the FISC has "vigorously defend[ed] the interests customarily protected by the Fourth Amendment."[90]

Robert J. Delahunty, *The Fourth Amendment Goes to War*.[91] Delahanty defends the October 23, 2001 memorandum by the White House's Office of Legal Counsel, prepared by Delahanty and John C. Yoo, which opined that warrantless searches and seizures of suspected foreign terrorists within the United States by military authorities would not violate the Fourth Amendment when ordered by the President or another high executive branch official.[92] Delahunty contends that the warrant requirement and probable cause requirement of the Fourth Amendment do not apply to searches and seizures of suspected foreign terrorists by the military (as opposed to searches by civilian law enforcement officials).[93]

---

[86] 91 MINN. L. REV. 1209 (May 2007).

[87] *Id.* at 1216-60 (providing a history of practice under FISA before 9/11, then examining the post-9/11 applications of the Foreign Intelligence Purpose rule, the development of the Terrorist Surveillance Program, and the collapse of the so-called wall between different intelligence agencies and between intelligence and law enforcement functions).

[88] *Id.* at 1280-84 (discussing proposed amendments to FISA and considering "Can FISA Be Saved"?)

[89] 2016 B.Y.U. L. REV. 771 (2016).

[90] *Id.* at 775; *see also* Emily Berman, *The Two Faces of the Foreign Intelligence Court*, 91 INDIANA L. J. 1191 (2016) (also defending the FISC).

[91] 10 ENGAGE: J. OF FEDERALIST SOC'Y PRACTICE GROUPS 107 (2009).

[92] *Id.* at 107-08.

[93] *Id.* at 108.

Owen Fiss, & Trevor Sutton, A WAR LIKE NO OTHER: THE CONSTITUTION IN A TIME OF TERROR (2015).[94] Fiss and Sutton contend that the federal government has violated the Fourth Amendment in its use of FISA and similar extra-statutory surveillance programs (such as the Terrorist Surveillance Program during the George W. Bush Administration). They contend that "[t]he legislators must go back to the drawing board and come up with a statute confined to investigations about international terrorism."[95]

Tracey Maclin, *The Bush Administration's Terrorist Surveillance Program and the Fourth Amendment Warrant Requirement: Lessons from Justice Powell and the* Keith *Case.*[96] Maclin argues that the George W. Bush Administration's Terrorist Surveillance Program involving warrantless electronic surveillance of communications between American citizens and persons abroad suspected of having connections with foreign terrorist groups violated the Fourth Amendment. [97]

Richard A. Posner, NOT A SUICIDE PACT: THE CONSTITUTION IN A TIME OF NATIONAL EMERGENCY (2006). Posner contends that the current statutory regime governing the federal government's surveillance powers concerning national security and terrorism is inadequate.[98] He proposes, among other things, that "the government could, in the present emergency [following the 9/11 terrorist attacks], intercept *all* electronic communications inside or outside the United States, of citizens as well as foreigners, without being deemed to violate the Fourth Amendment, provided that computers were used to winnow the gathered data, blocking human inspection of

---

[94] *See id.* at 225-258 (Chapter 9: "Warrantless Wiretapping") (discussing governmental violations of the Fourth Amendment through the use of FISA and other surveillance programs).

[95] *Id.* at 257; *see also* Owen Fiss, *Even in a Time of Terror*, 31 YALE L. & POL'Y REV. 1 (2012) (making the same argument).

[96] 41 U.C. DAVIS L. REV. 1259 (2008).

[97] *Id.* at 1293-96.

[98] *See generally id.* at 31-51 (Chapter Two: "How Does National Security Shape Constitutional Rights?"); *id.* at 77, 87-103 (Chapter Four: "Rights Against Brutal Interrogation, and Against Searches and Seizure").

intercepted communications that contained no clues of terrorist activity."[99]

Robert C. Power, *"Intelligence" Searches and Purpose: A Significant Mismatch Between Constitutional Criminal Procedure and the Law of Intelligence-Gathering*.[100] Power discusses the amendments to FISA following the 9/11 terrorist attacks and the federal government's "foreign intelligence" searches and use of evidence discovered during such surveillance in criminal prosecutions of terrorists.[101]

Ronald J. Sievert, *Time to Rewrite the Ill-Conceived and Dangerous Foreign Intelligence Surveillance Act of 1978*.[102] Sievert contends that Congress, in conformity with the Fourth Amendment, should amend FISA to lower the standard of proof to "reasonable suspicion" (from its present "probable cause") for court orders authorizing surveillance of targets in the U.S. or abroad who may be planning to use a weapon of mass destruction or who is the subject of an authorization for use of military force.[103] He also proposes that the evidentiary fruits of such searches should be limited to criminal prosecutions for terrorism or national security offenses.[104]

Glenn Sulmasy & John Yoo, <u>Katz</u> *and the War on Terrorism*.[105] Sulmasy and Yoo contend that, although the Supreme Court's modern Fourth Amendment doctrine, first announced in *Katz v. United States* (1967) properly applies to law enforcement searches related to domestic criminal activity, *Katz* should have no application to executive branch searches that seek to prevent international terrorism in the United States.[106] The authors also are critical of what they deem to be the unnecessarily "cumbersome" procedures required by FISA and also defend the Terrorist Surveillance Program (TSP) conducted

---

[99] *Id.* at 99-100; *see also* Richard A. Posner, *Privacy, Surveillance, and Law*, 75 U. CHI. L. REV. 245 (2008).

[100] 30 PACE L. REV. 620 (2010).

[101] *Id.* at 646-53.

[102] 3 NAT'L SEC. L. J. 47 (2014).

[103] *Id.* at 47-48.

[104] *Id.* at 99.

[105] 41 U.C. DAVIS L. REV. 1219 (2008).

[106] *Id.* at 1235-43.

during the George W. Bush Administration as not having violated the Fourth Amendment.[107]

Peter P. Swire, *The System of Foreign Intelligence Law.*[108] Swire offers an analysis of the history and theory of the U.S. system of foreign intelligence surveillance law and provides proposals for reform of the post-9/11 system.[109]

Patrick Walsh, *Stepping On (or Over) the Constitution's Line: Evaluating FISA Section 702 in a World of Changing "Reasonableness" Under the Fourth Amendment.*[110] Walsh discusses section 702 of FISA —which allows the federal government to engage in warrantless surveillance of foreign nationals on foreign soi— and, in particular, addresses whether section 702 violates the Fourth Amendment.[111] He concludes that "a future court [likely will] determine that FISA section 702 is an unconstitutional search under the Fourth Amendment."[112]

II.   PHYSICAL SEIZURES AND SEARCHES TO DETER AND PREVENT TERRORISM

Another recurring Fourth Amendment issue in the context of terrorism and national security is law enforcement officers' warrantless physical seizures and searches, such as roadblocks and mass searches of members of the public in the context of public transportation or public venues such as sporting events. Such searches and seizures raise two related but distinct Fourth Amendment questions—whether they require a search warrant and whether they require any level of individualized suspicion (probable cause or at least "reasonable suspicion"). The primary issue is whether there should be a "terrorism exception" to the warrant and probable cause requirements or, instead, whether such warrantless

---

[107] *See also* John C. Yoo, *The Terrorist Surveillance Program and the Constitution,* 14 GEO. MASON L. REV. 565 (2007) (contending that the Terrorist Surveillance Program was a valid exercise of the President's powers as commander-in-chief and did not violate the Fourth Amendment because such anti-terrorism searches are "reasonable").

[108] 72 GEO. WASH. L. REV. 1306 (2004)

[109] *Id.*

[110] 18 N.Y.U. J. LEGIS. & PUB. POL'Y 741 (2015)

[111] *Id.* at 782.

[112] *Id.* at 793.

searches and seizures fall within an established exception, such as the "special needs" exception.[113]

The following cases and scholarly works have addressed the constitutionality of warrantless physical searches and seizures seeking to deter and prevent terrorism.

A. Selected Case Law

Edmond v. City of Indianapolis.[114] In a case in which the Court held that a warrantless "drug interdiction" roadblock violated the Fourth Amendment, the Court noted in dicta that:

> [T]he Fourth Amendment would almost certainly permit an appropriately tailored [warrantless] roadblock set up to thwart an imminent terrorist attack or to catch a dangerous criminal who is likely to flee by way of a particular route.... The exigencies created by these scenarios are far removed from the circumstances under which authorities might simply stop cars as a matter, of course, to see if there just happens to be a felon leaving the jurisdiction. While we do not limit the purposes that may justify a checkpoint program to any rigid set of categories, we decline to approve a program whose primary purpose is ultimately indistinguishable from the general interest in crime control.[115]

Florida v. JL.[116] In a case in which the Court held that the warrantless stop and frisk of a defendant based solely on an anonymous tip that he possessed a firearm violated the Fourth Amendment, the Court stated:

---

[113] *See, e.g.,* Chandler v. Miller, 520 U.S. 305, 313-14 (1997) (discussing the "special needs exception").

[114] 531 U.S. 32 (2000).

[115] *Id.* at 44 (refusing to suspend the usual requirement of individualized suspicion, in order to facilitate the search for the ever-present possibility that a motorist has committed some crime).

[116] 529 U.S. 266 (2000).

The facts of this case do not require us to speculate about the circumstances under which the danger alleged in an anonymous tip might be so great as to justify a search even without a showing of reliability. We do not say, for example, that a report of a person carrying a bomb need bear the indicia of reliability we demand for a report of a person carrying a firearm before the police can constitutionally conduct a frisk.[117]

Cassidy v. Chertoff.[118] In a civil rights action seeking to enjoin enforcement of the Maritime Transportation Security Act[119] as a violation of the Fourth Amendment, the Second Circuit held that the Act—which permitted the Coast Guard to conduct warrantless, suspicionless searches of vessels deemed potential targets of terrorism, including the personal property of passengers traveling on such vessels—passed muster under the Fourth Amendment "special needs" doctrine.[120] Despite passengers' interest in privacy in their baggage and other personal property brought aboard vessels, the government's interest in deterring and preventing terrorist attacks on large vessels carrying passengers outweighed the privacy interests.[121]

MacWade v. Kelly.[122] The Second Circuit rejected a Fourth Amendment challenge to New York City's program of warrantless, suspicionless searches of subway passenger's containers. The court concluded that the program fell within the "special needs" exception to the Fourth Amendment's warrant and probable cause requirements.[123]

---

[117] *Id*. at 274-75.

[118] 471 F.3d 67 (2d Cir. 2006).

[119] Pub. L. No. 107-295, 116 Stat. 2066 (2002).

[120] 471 F.3d at 82-84 (holding that it does not matter how great the risk is at a specific port, but the type of vessel is what is to be used to determine risk for terrorist attack).

[121] *Id*. at 76-77.

[122] 460 F.3d 260 (2d Cir. 2006).

[123] *Id*. at 263.

Johnson v. Tampa Sports Authority.[124] The district court refused to vacate a preliminary injunction against a public authority's policy requiring pat-down searches of all ticket holders seeking to attend Tampa Bay Buccaneers games.[125] The court concluded such warrantless, suspicionless seizures and searches violated the Fourth Amendment.[126] On appeal, the Eleventh Circuit concluded that there was no Fourth Amendment violation because the plaintiffs consented to the search as a condition of entry into the stadium.[127]

Bourgeois v. Peters.[128] The Eleventh Circuit held that a municipal policy requiring all persons appearing at a public protest outside of a military base had to submit a metal detector and potential physical search by police violated the Fourth Amendment.[129] The court concluded that: "While the threat of terrorism is omnipresent, we cannot use it as the basis for restricting the scope of the Fourth Amendment's protections in any large gathering of people. In the absence of some reason to believe that international terrorists would target or infiltrate this protest, there is no basis for using September 11 as an excuse for searching the protestors."[130]

Commonwealth v. Carkhuff.[131] The court held that a state police policy of stopping all vehicles driving on the public roads near a public water reservoir, without a warrant or individualized suspicion, violated the Fourth Amendment because the police officers did not post any warning signs and did not set up a fixed checkpoint (so as to give drivers the opportunity to turn around and avoid the seizure and potential search).[132]

---

[124] 442 F. Supp. 2d 1257 (M.D. Fla. 2006), *vacated and remanded*, 530 F.3d 1320 (11th Cir. 2008).

[125] 442 F. Supp. 2d at 1258-59.

[126] *Id.* at 1259 (holding the searches violated both the Fourth Amendment and the Florida Constitution).

[127] 530 F.3d 1322-23.

[128] 387 F.3d 1303 (11th Cir. 2004).

[129] *Id.* at 1307 (stating that there were mootness, First Amendment, and Fourth Amendment considerations for failing to uphold the lower court's decision).

[130] *Id.* at 1311 (noting that while the threat of terrorism is omnipresent, it cannot be used as an at will excuse for restricting the scope of the Fourth Amendment).

[131] 804 N.E.2d 317 (Mass. 2004).

[132] *Id.* at 130.

United States v. Green.[133]   The Fifth Circuit rejected a Fourth Amendment challenge to a warrantless, suspicionless search of every sixth car entering a military base on the ground that the base's commander's rationale of deterring terrorism was reasonable under the Fourth Amendment.[134]

United States v. Edwards.[135] The Second Circuit rejected a Fourth Amendment challenge to the Federal Aviation Administration's suspicionless, warrantless search of airline travelers' luggage claiming the government's interest in preventing airline hijackings and bombings was compelling and also that passengers were given notice of the search as they entered the line to enter the airport.[136]

B.   *Leading Legal Scholarship*

Derek M. Alphran, *Changing Tides: A Lesser Expectation of Privacy in a Post 9/11 World*.[137] Alphran is critical of the what he perceives as a steady erosion of Fourth Amendment protections in connection with anti-terrorism searches since the 9/11 terrorist attacks.[138]

Geoffrey S. Corn, *Terrorism, Tips, and the Touchstone of Reasonableness: Seeking a Balance Between Threat Response and Privacy Dilution*.[139] Corn proposes a Fourth Amendment rule applicable to non-predictive anonymous tips about an imminent terrorist attack: allow for warrantless searches and seizures of the suspected person or place yet limit the admissibility of any incriminating evidence discovered to evidence related to the threat that triggered the search.[140]

---

[133] 293 F.3d 855 (5th Cir. 2002).

[134] *Id.* at 862.

[135] 498 F.2d 496 (2d Cir. 1974).

[136] *Id.* at 498.

[137] Derek M. Alphran, *Changing Tides: A Lesser Expectation of Privacy in a Post 9/11 World*, 13 RICH. J. L. & PUB. INT. 89 (2009).

[138] *Id.* at 95.

[139] Geoffrey S. Corn, *Terrorism, Tips, and the Touchstone of Reasonableness: Seeking a Balance Between Threat Response and Privacy* Dilution, 118 PENN ST. L. REV. 129 (2013).

[140] *Id.* at 141-44.

Anthony C. Coveny, *When the Immovable Object Meets the Unstoppable Force: Search and Seizure in the Age of Terrorism*.[141] Coveny discusses New York City's Container Inspection Program instituted after the 9/11 terrorist attacks and the Second Circuit decision that upheld that program against a Fourth Amendment challenge.[142]

Karly Jo Dixon, *The Special Needs Doctrine, Terrorism, and Reasonableness*.[143] Dixon contends that, in order for suspected terrorism to be a "special need," the threat must be real, substantial, imminent, and not primarily conventionally criminal. Furthermore, she contends, it must be shown that preventing the attack will be dangerously frustrated by the Fourth Amendment warrant and probable cause requirement.[144]

Scott Glick, *Consequence, Weapons of Mass Destruction, and the Fourth Amendment's "No-Win" Situation*.[145] Glick contends that, because weapons of mass destruction (WMD) such as nuclear or biological weapons did not exist when the Fourth Amendment was adopted in 1791, the Fourth Amendment must be interpreted to allow flexibility on the part of the federal government—that is, not being bound by traditional probable cause, warrant, and particularity requirements of the Fourth Amendment—in preventing terrorist attacks using WMD.[146] He proposes that Congress enact such legislation limited to catastrophic threats.[147]

Ronald M. Gould & Simon Stern, *Catastrophic Threats and the Fourth Amendment*.[148] Gould and Stern contend that the definition of "probable cause" should be redefined for purposes of searches for weapons of mass destruction (WMD).[149] In particular, they contend

---

[141] Anthony C. Coveny, *When the Immovable Object Meets the Unstoppable Force: Search and Seizure in the Age of* Terrorism, 31 AM. J. TRIAL ADVOC. 329 (2007).

[142] *Id.* at 331-33.

[143] Karly Jo Dixon, *The Special Needs Doctrine, Terrorism, and* Reasonableness, 21 TEX. J. ON C. L. & C. R. 35 (2015).

[144] *Id.*

[145] Scott Glick, *Consequence, Weapons of Mass Destruction, and the Fourth Amendment's "No-Win" Situation*, 90 IND. L. J. 1 (2015).

[146] *Id.* at 36.

[147] *Id.* at 40-44.

[148] Ronald M. Gould & Simon Stern, *Catastrophic Threats and the Fourth Amendment*, 77 SO. CAL. L. REV. 777 (2004).

[149] *Id.*

that the need for particularity, which normally is required for a finding of probable cause, should not apply to searches for WMD in a general area (as opposed to a specific locale) when reliable information supports the belief that a WMD is located somewhere in that general area.[150]

Kyle P. Hanson, *Suspicionless Terrorism Checkpoints Since 9/11: Searching for Uniformity*.[151] Hanson discusses the lower court cases addressing the constitutionality of warrantless, suspicionless antiterrorism checkpoints since the 9/11 terrorist attacks and notes that some of the decisions are conflicting.[152] He contends that such checkpoints are reasonable under the Fourth Amendment given the compelling government interest in deterring and preventing terrorism.[153] He additionally suggests that the "presence of attacks or threats of attacks in certain locales could lessen the quantum of specific information needed to justify searches in other areas," while admitting that safeguards are still essential.[154]

Charles J. Keeley III, *Subway Searches: Which Exception to the Warrant and Probable Cause Requirements Applies to Suspicionless Searches of Mass Transit Passengers to Prevent Terrorism?*.[155] Keeley contends that warrantless, suspicionless mass transit searches, such as the policy instituted in the New York City subway system after the 9/11 terrorist attacks, do not violate the Fourth Amendment.[156] However, unlike lower courts, which have usually upheld such mass searches under the Supreme Court's "special needs" doctrine, Keeley argues that the Supreme Court "should adopt a sui generis exception for antiterrorism mass transit searches in order to enable communities to defend themselves from this unique threat."[157]

---

[150] *Id.* at 787-88.

[151] 56 DRAKE L. REV. 171 (2007).

[152] *Id.* at 205-06 (noting that not only do courts differ on whether terrorism even qualifies as a special need, but also differ on what factors would make suspicionless searches constitutional).

[153] *Id.* at 209 (focusing on the relative successful use of such checkpoints in airports).

[154] *Id.* at 209-10.

[155] 74 FORDHAM L. REV. 3231 (2006).

[156] *Id.* at 3232.

[157] *Id.* (concluding first that other approaches fail to address all facets of the issue and instead pose a threat to Fourth Amendment protections).

Ric Simmons, *Searching for Terrorists: Why Public Safety Is Not a Special Need*.[158] Simmons proposes that warrantless, suspicionless antiterrorism searches be permitted as reasonable searches under the Fourth Amendment so long as the evidentiary fruits of such searches are inadmissible in a criminal prosecution.[159]

III. DEFINITIONAL ISSUE AND CONSIDERATION OF SUSPECTS' RACE, ETHNICITY, OR RELIGION

A. Threshold Issue: Defining "Terrorism"

Norman Abrams, *Terrorism Prosecutions in U.S. Federal Court: Exceptions to Constitutional Evidence Rules and the Development of a Cabined Exception for Coerced Confessions*.[160] Abrams contends that a "terrorism" definition should require actual or threatened serious violent acts intended "to intimidate or coerce a civilian population" or "influence the policy of a government by intimidation or coercion" and "in furtherance of political or social objectives."[161] The exception should not distinguish between international and domestic terrorism and should apply equally to U.S. citizen suspects as well as non-citizens.[162]

Alex Schmid, *Terrorism – The Definitional Problem*.[163] Schmit offers a detailed discussion of how "terrorism" has been defined in a wide variety of contexts, inside and outside the United States, and over time.[164]

Ryan J. Sydejko, *International Influence on Democracy: How Terrorism Exploited a Deteriorating Fourth Amendment*.[165] Sydejko discusses different definitions of "terrorism," including those outlined in 18 U.S.C. § 2331 and 6 U.S.C. § 101(15).[166] He argues that "[a]n

---

[158] 59 DUKE L. J. 843 (2010).

[159] *Id*. at 915-21.

[160] 4 HARV. NAT'L SEC. J. 58, 120-21 (2012).

[161] *Id*. at 121-22.

[162] *Id*. at 121.

[163] 36 CASE W. RES. J. INT'L L. 375 (2004).

[164] *Id*. (including in his discussion tables outlining the commonalities between and elements of the definitions of terrorism widely used).

[165] 7 J. LAW IN SOC'Y 220, 255-59 (2006).

[166] 18 U.S.C. § 2331 (2012); 6 U.S.C. § 101(15) (2012).

unambiguous definition of terrorism is vital if America is to continue curtailing liberties in the 'War on Terror.'"[167]

B. Constitutionality of Considering Race, Ethnicity, or Religion of a Suspected Terrorist

United States v. Martinez-Fuerte.[168] In a case in which the Court rejected a Fourth Amendment challenge to a warrantless, suspicionless immigration checkpoint near the U.S.-Mexican border, the Court stated: "We further believe that it is constitutional to refer motorists selectively to the secondary inspection area at the San Clemente checkpoint on the basis of criteria that would not sustain a roving-patrol stop. Thus, even if it be assumed that such referrals are made largely on the basis of apparent Mexican ancestry, we perceive no constitutional violation." [169]

United States v. Brignoni-Ponce.[170] In a case in which the Court held that a "roving border patrol" traveling near the U.S.-Mexican border stopped a car based solely on the apparent Mexican ancestry of the car's occupants violated the Fourth Amendment, the Court stated:

> In this case[,] the officers relied on a single factor to justify stopping [the] respondent's car: the apparent Mexican ancestry of the occupants. We cannot conclude that this furnished reasonable grounds to believe that the three occupants were aliens. At best the officers had only a fleeting glimpse of the persons in the moving car, illuminated by headlights. Even if they saw enough to think that the occupants were of Mexican descent, this factor alone would justify neither a reasonable belief that they were aliens nor a reasonable belief that the car concealed other aliens who were illegally in the country. Large numbers of native-born and naturalized citizens have the physical characteristics identified with Mexican

---

[167] 7 J. LAW IN SOC'Y at 259.

[168] 428 U.S. 543, 653-64 (1976).

[169] *Id.* (stating further that the intrusion in this case was "sufficiently minimal that no particularized reason need exist to justify it.").

[170] 422 U.S. 873, 885-87 (1975).

ancestry, and even in the border area[,] a relatively small proportion of them are aliens. The likelihood that any given person of Mexican ancestry is an alien is high enough to make Mexican appearance a relevant factor but standing alone it does not justify stopping all Mexican-Americans to ask if they are aliens.[171]

United States v. Montero-Camargo.[172] In this case, the Ninth Circuit refused to follow what it deemed non-binding dicta in *Martinez-Fuerte* and *Brignoni-Ponce*:

[W]e conclude that, at this point in our nation's history, and given the continuing changes in our ethnic and racial composition, Hispanic appearance is, in general, of such little probative value that it may not be considered as a relevant factor where particularized or individualized suspicion is required. Moreover, we conclude, for the reasons we have indicated, that it is also not an appropriate factor.[173]

Samuel R. Gross & Debra Livingston, *Racial Profiling Under Attack.*[174] Gross and Livingston discuss racial and ethnic profiling since 9/11 and focus, in particular, on the Justice Department's 2001 interviews of thousands of Middle Eastern men from countries with a strong al Qaeda presence who were in the United States less than two years.[175] They contend that such interviews were not racial or ethnic "profiling" given the particular circumstances following the 9/11 terrorist attacks, yet also contend that there should be a "strong

---

[171] *Id.* (noting a concern that the "legitimate needs of law enforcement" did not rise to a level requiring such an interference with general traffic).

[172] 208 F.3d 1122, 1135 (9th Cir. 2000).

[173] *Id.* (stating that while deciding a narrow constitutional question, generally allowing race to be a factor would send a message to individuals who are not white that they have fewer rights).

[174] 102 COLUM. L. REV. 1413 (2002).

[175] *Id.* at 1417-18.

presumption that no racial or ethnic group should be considered more suspicious or dangerous than any other."[176]

R. Richard Banks, *Racial Profiling and Antiterrorism Efforts*.[177] Banks discusses what he deems a difficult question of whether law enforcement's focus on Arabs and Muslims in the United States who came from Middle Eastern countries after the 9/11 terrorist attacks constituted improper racial, ethnic, or religious "profiling."[178] He contends that such a focus "straddle[d] the boundary separating [legitimate focus on suspects based on descriptions of their race or ethnicity] and profiling."[179]

Kevin R. Johnson, *How Racial Profiling in America Became the Law of the Land: United States v. Brignoni-Ponce and Whren v United States and the Need for Truly Rebellious Lawyering*.[180] Johnson argues that Supreme Court decisions in the decades before the 9/11 terrorist attacks effectively authorized racial profiling by law enforcement officials, but that there was a growing movement to curtail such profiling.[181] He further contends that the 9/11 terrorist attacks "noticeably slowed" the movement against racial profiling by law enforcement.[182]

Deborah A. Ramirez et al., *Defining Racial Profiling in a Post-September 11 World*.[183] Ramirez and her co-authors discuss racial and religious profiling by law enforcement, both before and after the 9/11 terrorist attacks, and contend that "racial or religious profiling" both violates civil liberties and also "is neither necessary nor effective in the War on Terrorism."[184]

---

[176] *Id.* at 1438 (arguing that the use of race in "profiling" has wider negative implications to the profiled group such as humiliation and spreading misleading information about said group, complicating attempts to balance the use of race as a primary factor in investigations).

[177] 89 CORNELL L. REV. 1201 (2004).

[178] *Id.* at 1207-17.

[179] *Id.* at 1202.

[180] 98 GEO. L. J. 1005 (2010).

[181] *Id.* at 1015-25.

[182] *Id.* at 1076.

[183] 40 AM. CRIM. L. REV. 1195 (2003).

[184] *Id.* at 1195-96 (focusing on an argument that racial or religious profiling actually negatively impacts investigations, rather than helping them, because it keeps investigators from "digging deeper" and focusing on other techniques such as behavioral analysis and "suspect- or crime-specific descriptions").

IV. CONCLUSION

This essay has offered a brief sketch of the leading judicial decisions and scholarly works addressing the extent to which the Fourth Amendment applies to searches and seizures related to suspected terrorists and others who may threaten national security. Despite the importance of this issue, the Supreme Court has yet to offer clear guidance to the lower courts, policymakers, and law enforcement concerning any limitations erected by the Fourth Amendment in the context of such searches and seizures.

FLYING GUNS: FEDERAL REGULATORY POWER VS. STATES & THE SECOND AMENDMENT

By Prescott A. Heighton*

INTRODUCTION

In 2015, a disturbing new trend in recreational civil aviation took flight: national news was covering, for the first time, a story about an armed recreational drone.[1] Austin Haughwout, a then 18-year-old college student, posted a video on YouTube of a lightweight recreational drone that he had modified to mount and fire a semi-automatic handgun.[2] Currently, there are no federal laws that make it illegal for someone to arm a recreational drone,[3] nor does the

---

* *Prescott Heighton is a 2019 J.D./M.A. candidate at the American University Washington College of Law and the American University School of International Service. He also currently serves as the Editor-in-Chief for the American University National Security Law Brief.*

[1] Michael Martinez, *Handgun-firing drone appears legal in video, but FAA, police probe further*, CNN (Jul 21, 2015, 8:15 PM), https://www.cnn.com/2015/07/21/us/gun-drone-connecticut/index.html (reporting after a controversial video showing Mr. Haughwout's drone firing a gun several times); *see also Is teen's homemade "flying gun" illegal?*, CBS NEWS (Jul. 23 2015, 7:05 AM), https://www.cbsnews.com/ news/homemade-drone-mounted-semi-automatic-handgun-may-not-be-illegal-law-enforcement-say/.

[2] *Id.* *See also* Victoria Bekiempis, *No Word Yet on Whether Gun-Firing Drone Inventor Broke FAA Rules*, NEWSWEEK (Jul. 25, 2015, 2:42 PM), http://www.newsweek.com/no-word-gun-firing-drone-inventor-broke-aviation-law-357063 (stating that ATF had reviewed the video and did not believe that the armed drone violated any existing firearm regulations). A handgun is defined as "a firearm which has a short stock and is designed to be held and fired by the use of a single hand[.]" 18 U.S.C. § 921(a)(29) (2012). A semiautomatic handgun in the context of this incident also falls within the definition provided by the Code of Federal Regulations for 'semiautomatic pistol,' in that a "[s]emiautomatic pistol [refers to] [a]ny repeating pistol which utilizes a portion of the energy of a firing cartridge to extract the fired cartridge case and chamber the next round, and which requires a separate pull of the trigger to fire each cartridge." 27 C.F.R. § 478.11 (2018).

[3] Jason Koebler, *Arming Your Drone Is Legal: Only States have the authority to make homemade gun drones illegal*, MOTHERBOARD (Jun. 10, 2016, 6:09 PM), https://motherboard.vice.com/en us/article/yp33ag/arming-your-drone-is-legal [hereinafter *Arming Your Drone is Legal*] (describing the limits of the federal regulatory scheme and its current inability to ban weaponized

Federal Aviation Administration (FAA) have the vested regulatory authority to prohibit these flying weapons.[4] The FAA only has vested authority to regulate the national airspace regarding use, management and efficiency, air traffic control, safety, and aircraft noise.[5] However, the lack of federal legislation and regulation does not mean that armed recreational drones do not present a clear danger to national security and public safety.

Some States have already taken steps to address this danger by enacting laws and regulations that would make these weaponized aircraft illegal in their jurisdictions.[6] This approach has resulted in a patchwork of regulation that poses an obvious problem by presenting clear gaps that could be exploited by criminals and terrorists. Therefore, to deal with this emergent threat, it is incumbent upon Congress to pass new legislation expanding the FAA's vested

---

recreational drones).

[4] *Id.* (citing Jim Williams, a former head of the FAA's drone office, who stated that the FAA's 2015 UAS fact sheet tells States that the FAA does not have the power to regulate armed drones and it is therefore up to each state).

[5] 49 U.S.C. §§ 40103, 44502, 44701-44735 (2011); *see* State and Local Regulation of Unmanned Aircraft Systems (UAS) Fact Sheet, FEDERAL AVIATION ADMINISTRATION OFFICE OF THE CHIEF COUNSEL (Dec. 17, 2015), https://www.faa.gov/uas/resources/uas_regulations_policy/media/uas_fact_sheet_final.pdf [hereinafter 2015 UAS Fact Sheet].

[6] Koebler, *supra* note 3 (providing the examples of Nevada, North Carolina, Oregon, Vermont, and Wisconsin as States that, as of June 2016, had passed legislation that provide some limits on arming drones). As of 2018, 44 States have enacted laws or adopted regulations concerning the use of UAS. Current Unmanned Aircraft State Law Landscape, NATIONAL CONFERENCE OF STATE LEGISLATURES (Feb. 1, 2018), http://www.ncsl.org/research/transportation/current-unmanned-aircraft-state-law-landscape.aspx. *See also* 2016 Unmanned Aircraft Systems (UAS) State Legislation Update, NATIONAL CONFERENCE OF STATE LEGISLATURES (Mar. 20, 2017), http://www.ncsl.org/research/transportation/2016-unmanned-aircraft-systems-uas-state-legislation-update.aspx ("Ten States—Arizona, California, Delaware, Kansas, Louisiana, Michigan, Oregon, Tennessee, Utah and Vermont—created new criminal offenses in 2016. States particularly focused on criminal classification of UAS interface with emergency services, *UAS weaponization* and other offenses such as reckless aircraft operation and using a drone to conduct surveillance of critical infrastructure. . . . *Five States*—Nevada, North Carolina, Oregon, Vermont and Wisconsin—*prohibit the possession or use of a weaponized drone by anyone.*") (emphasis added).

authority to include aircraft—manned and unmanned—carrying weapons and hazardous materials.

This paper will begin by first providing a brief background that will lay out the current regulatory authorities of the Federal Aviation Administration and its posture towards regulating armed recreational drones. Part I will also contain a brief discussion of State police powers. This section will conclude with an examination of the basic protections provided by the right to bear arms under the Second Amendment to the United States Constitution. Part II will analyze whether Congress could legislate a ban that prevents the arming of recreational drones, given that armed civilian drones are a clear national security and public safety threat and likely have no justifiable legal basis to permit their usage. This part will then discuss how legislation such as the *No Armed Drones Act of 2017* would resolve this gap in the current law. Part III will conclude by analyzing the *No Armed Drones Act* and whether it is a viable Federal solution to resolve the national security threat posed by weaponized drones.

I. BACKGROUND

Government fears of armed recreational drones have been around for some years now, and armed drones are something that various agencies in the national and homeland security realms have been actively trying to address.[7] The reason why efforts to address this threat vector are underway should be somewhat obvious: imagine a world in the near future where no legislation has been enacted to

---

[7] *See* W. J. Hennigan, *Experts Say Drones Pose a National Security Threat – and We Aren't* Ready, TIME (May 31, 2018), http://time.com/5295586/drones-threat/ (stating that the Department of Defense plans to spend $401.2 million o counter-drone initiatives in FY2018, and quoting Department of Homeland Security Secretary, Kirstjen Nielsen, saying, "We know that terrorists are using drones overseas to advance plots and attacks, and we've already seen criminals use them along and within our borders for illicit purposes. . . . We are working with Congress for the authorities needed to ensure we can better protect the American people against emerging drone threats."); Kevin Poulsen, *Why the US Government is Terrified of Hobbyist Drones*, WIRED (Feb. 5, 2015, 5:15 AM), https://www.wired.com/2015/02/white-house-drone/ (providing insight into a 2015 conference held in Arlington, Virginia and hosted by the U.S. military, Department of Homeland Security, and FAA to discuss the dangerous potential of terrorists arming hobbyist drones to conduct attacks or assassinations).

remedy the security threat posed by armed recreational drones, only to have a terrorist use such a drone to conduct a D.C. Sniper-style attack.[8] Thus, there is an obvious gap, but why does it exist, and why can that gap only be closed by new legislation? The answer lies with the powers given by Congress to the FAA.

A. *The current federal regulatory scheme*

In 2015, the FAA's Office of Chief Counsel published its *State and Local Regulation of Unmanned Aircraft Systems (UAS) Fact Sheet*.[9] The FAA's interpretation of its vested authorities is stated within but can be summarized as directing the creation of a "consistent regulatory system for aircraft and use of airspace . . . [t]o ensure the maintenance of a safe and sound air transportation system[.]"[10] The focus is on air safety, and ensuring a regulatory scheme that is consistent across the national airspace.[11]

The FAA then laid out its regulatory posture concerning drones in the next section of the *Fact Sheet*.[12] Pursuant to sections 332 and 333 of the *FAA Modernization and Reform Act of 2012*,[13] the FAA proposed (and later adopted)[14] "a framework of regulations that would allow routine commercial use of certain small UAS in today's aviation

---

[8] *See Is teen's homemade "flying gun" illegal?*, *supra* note 1.

[9] *See* 2015 UAS Fact Sheet, *supra* note 5 (outlining the FAA's assessment of its regulatory authorities in the context of unmanned aerial systems).

[10] *Id.* at 2.

[11] *Id.* Black's Law Dictionary defines "national airspace" as "[t]he pillar of air above a country's territory—including internal waters and the territorial sea—over which it has complete and exclusive sovereignty and through which foreign aircraft have no right of innocent passage." *National airspace*, BLACK'S LAW DICTIONARY (10th ed. 2014). *See also* Convention on International Civil Aviation art. 1, Dec. 7, 1944, 61 Stat. 1180, 15 U.N.T.S. 295 (recognizing that "every State has complete and exclusive sovereignty over the airspace above its territory.").

[12] *See* 2015 UAS Fact Sheet, *supra* note 5.

[13] *See id.*; FAA Modernization and Reform Act of 2012, Pub. L. No. 112-95, §§ 332, 333, 126 Stat. 11, 73-76, (2012).

[14] *See* FEDERAL AVIATION ADMINISTRATION, FACT SHEET — SMALL UNMANNED AIRCRAFT REGULATIONS (PART 107) (2018), https://www.faa.gov/news/fact_sheets/news_story.cfm?newsId=22615&cid=TW637.

system, while maintaining flexibility to accommodate future technological innovations."[15]

Section 333(b) does mandate that the Secretary of Transportation need to determine whether the operational capabilities of the drones that would be regulated posed "a hazard to users of the national airspace system or the public or [present] a threat to national security"[16] before deciding to regulate instead of banning their usage outright.[17] However, likely as a result of how drones were being operated at the time, the FAA did not conclude that drones presented such a threat to public safety, the safety of air navigation, or national security that it warranted a ban on their operation, and decided to regulate them instead.[18] The only provision of the existing regulations that may allow the FAA to ban the usage of weaponized recreational drones is the prohibition against hazardous operation, but that would only be if the drone operator was operating it in a manner dangerous to life or property and that is also careless or reckless.[19] However, for

---

[15] 2015 UAS Fact Sheet, *supra* note 5, at 2.

[16] FAA Modernization and Reform Act of 2012 § 333 (b)(1), Pub. L. 112-95, 126 Stat. 11 (2012).

[17] *See* 2015 UAS Fact Sheet, *supra* note 5, at 2 (stating that under section 333 of the FAA Modernization and Reform Act of 2012, Congress directed the Secretary of Transportation to assess the impact of drones operating in the national airspace system on public risk and national security before adopting any regulations).

[18] *See* 2015 UAS Fact Sheet, *supra* note 5, at 2 (pointing out this requirement, but then moving on to talking about FAA regulations that could have resulted only after making the determination that these systems did not pose a substantial enough risk to warrant a ban).

[19] *See* 14 C.F.R. § 107.23 (2018) ("No person may: (a) Operate a small unmanned aircraft system in a careless or reckless manner so as to endanger the life or property of another"). Likely because it focuses on the conduct of the activity and not the legality of the armed drone itself, pursing this avenue is probably quite feasible according to law enforcement experts and Second Amendment rights advocates alike. *See* Martinez, https://www.cnn.com/2015/07/21/us/gun-drone-connecticut/index.html (providing the opinion of law enforcement analyst Tom Fuentes under the section "Reckless conduct?"); *Arming Your Drone is Legal, supra* note 3 (quoting Jim Williams, former head of the FAA's drone office); Jason Koebler, *The Next Gun Debate? Armed Drones Could Be Protected By the Second Amendment*, U.S. NEWS & WORLD REPORT (May 21, 2013, 5:20 PM), https://www.usnews.com/news/articles/2013/05/21/the-next-gun-debate-armed-drones-could-be-protected-

this to be used effectively, it would first have to be determined that Congress intended for the federal government to entirely occupy the field, thereby preempting state regulations.[20]

B. State police powers and aviation

The United States Constitution provides that the "laws of the United States . . . shall be the supreme law of the land[.]"[21] The Supremacy Clause creates a basis for courts to find that federal law preempts local and state laws and regulations when Congress intends for a law—or a regulation based on the authority granted by law to an agency—to preempt those laws and regulations.[22] However, if the

---

by-the-second-amendment [hereinafter *The Next Gun Debate?*] (quoting the concerns of Dave Workman, a representative for the Citizens Committee for the Right to Keep and Bear Arms). An argument could similarly be made that the FAA regulation prohibiting pilots from allowing objects that create a hazard to persons or property to be "dropped" from an aircraft under their control, thereby prohibiting them from firing a weapon attached to or from the inside of an aircraft if such actions are taken with disregard to the hazard posed to life or property. 14 C.F.R. § 91.15 (2018).

[20] *See* Arizona v. United States, 567 U.S. 387, 401 (2012) ("Where Congress occupies an entire field . . . even complimentary state regulation is impermissible. Field preemption reflects a congressional decision to foreclose any state regulation in the area, even if it is parallel to federal standards.")

[21] U.S. CONST. art. VI, cl. 2.

[22] *See* Wardair Canada, Inc. v. Florida Dept. of Revenue, 477 U.S. 1, 6 (1986) ("The Supremacy Clause . . . confirms that when Congress legislates within the scope of its constitutionally granted powers, that legislation may displace state law . . . ."); Silkwood v. Kerr-McGee Corp., 464 U.S. 238, 248 (1984) ("If Congress evidences an intent to occupy a given field, any state law falling within that field is preempted."); Pacific Gas & Electric v. State Energy Resources Conservation & Dev. Commission, 461 U.S. 190, 203-04 (1983) ("It is well-established that within Constitutional limits Congress may preempt state authority by so stating in express terms. . . . Absent explicit preemptive language, Congress' intent to supercede state law altogether may be found from a 'scheme of federal regulation so pervasive as to make reasonable the inference that Congress left no room to supplement it,' 'because the Act of Congress may touch a field in which the federal interest is so dominant that the federal system will be assumed to preclude enforcement of state laws on the same subject,' or because 'the object sought to be obtained by the federal law and the character of obligations imposed by it may reveal the same purpose.'"); Rice v. Santa Fe Elevator Corp., 331 U.S. 218, 236 (1947)

federal government does not express its intent to occupy the field fully, then the States maintain authority in that field except for those authorities provided to the federal government by the Constitution.[23] This is especially the case in areas, such as police powers, that are traditionally assumed to be within the power of the state.[24]

In theory, "[t]he United States Government has exclusive sovereignty of airspace of the United States,"[25] but in practice, the courts have approached the field of aviation on a case-by-case basis with the understanding that Congress has not expressed a general preemption in the field.[26] Regarding this particular issue, the FAA has

---

("Congress can act so unequivocally as to make clear that it intends no regulation except its own."); Bethlehem Steel Co. v. New York State Lab. Board, 330 U.S. 767, 773-74 (1947) ("Congress has passed statutes which initiate regulation of certain activities, but where effective regulation must wait upon the issuance of rules by an administrative body. In the interval before those rules are established, this Court has usually held that the police power of the state may be exercised. . . . But when federal administration has made comprehensive regulations effectively governing the subject matter of the statute, the Court has said that a state regulation in the field of the statute is invalid even though that particular phase of the subject has not been taken up by the federal agency."). *See also* Montalvo v. Spirit Airlines, 508 F.3d 464, 471 (9th Cir. 2007) (applying the Supremacy Clause to regulations, whereby "when an agency administrator promulgates pervasive regulations pursuant to his Congressional authority, we may infer a preemptive intent unless it appears . . . that Congress would not have sanctioned the preemption.").
[23] *See* U.S. CONST. amend. X.
[24] Cipollone v. Liggett Grp., Inc., 505 U.S. 504, 516 (1992) ("Consideration of issues arising under the Supremacy Clause 'start[s] with the assumption that the historic police powers of the States [are] not to be superseded by . . . Federal Act unless that [is] the clear and manifest purpose of Congress'" (quoting *Rice*, 331 U.S. at 230)); *see also* Skysign Int'l, Inc. v. City and County of Honolulu, 276 F.3d 1109, 1115 (9th Cir. 2002) (stating that advertising in an area of regulation subject to the state's traditional police powers, and that unless the federal government had expressed a clear intent to occupy that field, then the state laws and regulations are not displaced); Garcia v. San Antonio Metropolitan Transit Authority, 469 U.S. 528, 549 (1985) ("The States unquestionably do retain a significant measure of sovereign authority. They do so, however, only to the extent (sic) that the Constitution has not divested them of their original powers and transferred those to the Federal Government.").
[25] 49 U.S.C. § 40103(a)(1) (2011).
[26] Braniff Airways, Inc. v. Nebraska State Bd. Of Equalization & Assessment,

interpreted that the powers vested in it by Congress do not occupy the police powers of the States,[27] specifically concerning law enforcement interests in aviation.[28] The FAA's guidance provided in the 2015 *Fact Sheet* uses the example of prohibitions against the attaching of weapons, such as firearms, to drones as a regulation or law that would be within the state government's police powers.[29]

C. *The Second Amendment and aircraft*

The law is far from clear on whether the Second Amendment protects the right of a pilot, owner, or operator of an aircraft to arm or weaponized it, but it is likely that such action is not permitted. The Second Amendment does not provide an unlimited, protected right that would abrogate a ban against arming a civilian aircraft.[30] Furthermore, the Supreme Court has stated that those weapons protected by the Second Amendment are those weapons that are in common use at the time.[31] Consequentially, those weapons not protected may be banned by Congress.[32] Armed aircraft—manned or unmanned—are clearly not weapons that are currently commonly possessed or used by civilians, and until these weapons are allowed to become articles of common use, they may still be controlled, regulated, or banned outright by Congress.[33]

---

347 U.S. 590, 595 (1954) ("The [Air Commerce] Act . . . did not expressly exclude the sovereign powers of the states.")

[27] *See Montalvo*, 508 F.3d at 471. If the FAA administrator believed that Congress had fully occupied the field of aviation and the national airspace, and, therefore, that the Administrator is vested with the power to regulate, then they would not have taken the stance that the States maintain their traditional police powers as they relate to the use of the sovereign airspace.

[28] *See* 2015 UAS Fact Sheet, *supra* note 5, at 3.

[29] *See id.*

[30] *See* District of Columbia v. Heller, 554 U.S. 570, 626 (2008) ("Like most rights, the right secured by the Second Amendment is not unlimited.")

[31] *Id.* at 624 (referencing *United States v. Miller*, 307 U.S. 174 (1939)).

[32] *Id.* at 624-25, 627 (discussing that weapons in "common use" at the time refers to those commonly possessed and used by civilians and does not include those other weapons commonly used by the military, civilian possession or use of which may lawfully be regulated, controlled, or banned by Congress).

[33] *See id. See also The Next Gun Debate?, supra* note 18 (providing commentary by Dan Terzian, author of *The Right to Bear (Robotic) Arms*, 117 PENN ST. L. REV.

II. ANALYSIS

Recognizing the supremacy of Federal law over State law in areas understood not to be implicitly or explicitly provided to the States by the Constitution, Congress would likely be able to legislate a ban on weaponized recreational drones due to their current uncommon possession or use by law-abiding civilians.[34] However, absent the permanent solution that new legislation would represent, it may still be possible for the Federal government to respond to known cases of drones used as weapons.

A. While the FAA might not have the power to regulate or respond to weaponized drones, that does not render the Federal government powerless

While the FAA does have two rules that may be used to address weaponized recreational drones—the hazardous operation rule under Part 107 (Small Unmanned Aircraft Systems) of Title 14 of the Code of Federal Regulations and Part 91's rule concerning the dropping of objects[35]—it runs into the issue of Congress not fully occupying the field of aviation. Without Congress placing all aspects of aviation, or at least those concerning drones, within the realm of federal law, it potentially leaves any regulation regarding public safety outside of the FAA's scope of authority.[36] While that may relegate the FAA to a backseat, there are (at least) two other Federal agencies that would have the authority to respond to cases of criminal misuse of weaponized drones: the Federal Bureau of Investigation (FBI) and the Bureau of Alcohol, Tobacco, Firearms, and Explosives (ATF).

Acts of terrorism are one of the chief concerns that arise out of the issue of weaponized drones.[37] While the likelihood of a terrorist attack using weaponized drones is still low, the threat is very real.[38]

---

775 (2013)).

[34] *See* discussion *supra* Part I.

[35] *See supra* note 18.

[36] *See* discussion *supra* Parts I.A, I.B.

[37] *See* Jana Winter, *What Would Happen if Terrorists Attacked the Super Bowl With Drones?*, FOREIGN POLICY (Feb. 3, 2018, 10:27 AM), http://foreignpolicy.com/2018/02/03/what-would-happen-if-terrorists-attacked-the-super-bowl-with-drones/.

[38] *See id.*; *Weaponized civilian drones a 'tangible reality'—US officials*, RT (last

Fortunately, due to domestic terrorism falling under the umbrella of Federal jurisdiction[39] the prevention of, and investigation into, domestic terrorist attacks has been handled primarily by the FBI.[40] While the FBI preventing prospective attacks and investigating actual ones is not the same as a proscriptive ban that prevents civilian possession of weaponized drones, it does at least allow for response to their criminal misuse under certain circumstances.

Additionally, depending on the type of weapon that is used to arm the drone, that weapon—and thereby possibly the weaponized drone as a weapons system[41]—could fall under the regulatory and law

---

edited Mar. 30, 2017, 10:39 AM), https://www.rt.com/usa/382745-weaponized-civilian-drones-tangible-reality/.

[39] *See* 18 U.S.C. §§ 2331–2339D (2018). For the purposes of this paper, the focus is on *domestic terrorism*, as defined in section 2331, wherein: "the term 'domestic terrorism' means activities that— (A) involve acts dangerous to human life and are a violation of the criminal laws of the United States or of any State; (B) appear to be intended– (i) to intimidate or coerce a civilian population; (ii) to influence policy of a government by intimidation or coercion; or (iii) to affect the conduct of a government by mass destruction, assassination, or kidnapping; and (C) occur primarily within the territorial jurisdiction of the United States. *Id.* § 2331.

[40] *See What We Investigate—Terrorism*, FEDERAL BUREAU OF INVESTIGATION, https://www.fbi.gov/investigate/ terrorism.

[41] A "weapons system" is generally defined as a "delivery mechanism for a weapon, especially a munition." *Weapons system*, WEAPONS LAW ENCYCLOPEDIA (last updated Nov. 30, 2013), http://weaponslaw.org/glossary/weapons-system. A more specific and useful definition has been provided by the United States Department of Defense which defines a weapons system as "[a] combination of one or more weapons with all related equipment, materials, services, personnel, and means of delivery and deployment (if applicable) required for self-sufficiency." *Id.* Another useful definition can be found on the website for the Weapons Law Encyclopedia, which, drawing on multiple sources, provides the following:

> A weapons system is a device or coordinated set of devices or objects that consists of one or more weapons and a means of delivery as well as integral equipment and materiel. A weapons system is distinguished from a weapon in that while it incorporates one or more weapons in many instances it can also be used for other purposes than killing, injuring, disorienting, or threatening a person or inflicting damage on a physical object. For instance, an aircraft can

enforcement authorities of the ATF.[42]   There is any number of proscribed weapons that civilians in the United States simply cannot possess, and there are many more that are regulated by the ATF.[43] For example, if a drone were modified such that it was armed with an unregistered modern machine gun (made after 1986), then pursuant to its authority under the Firearms Owners Protection Act of 1986, the ATF would be able to arrest that drone operator.[44]   As such, under certain circumstances, the Federal government would again be justified in its monitoring, prevention, and prosecution of criminals who arm drones in violation of Federal law.

B.   The No Armed Drones Act of 2017: Is it the solution?

For a more comprehensive solution that would prevent the weaponization of recreational drones, Congress must pass new legislation that would occupy the field and explicitly ban the

---

conduct surveillance and a ship can transport personnel and materiel. *Id.*

[42] *National Firearms Act*, BUREAU OF ALCOHOL, TOBACCO, FIREARMS, AND EXPLOSIVES (last reviewed Apr. 26, 2018), https://atf.gov/rules-and-regulations/national-firearms-act (providing an overview of the applicable laws and noting that the ATF has jurisdiction over the unlawful possession of certain firearms and destructive devices). *See also About,* BUREAU OF ALCOHOL, TOBACCO, FIREARMS, AND EXPLOSIVES (last visited Jul. 28, 2018), https://atf.gov/about (stating the mission of the ATF as "protect[ing] the public from crimes involving firearms, explosives, arson, and the diversion of alcohol and tobacco products; regulates lawful commerce in firearms and explosives; and provides worldwide support to law enforcement, public safety, and industry partners.")

[43] *See generally* Machine Guns, Destructive Devices, and Certain Other Firearms, 27 C.F.R. Part 479 (2018). *See also* 18 U.S.C. §§ 921–931 (2011); 26 U.S.C. §§ 5801–5872 (2011).

[44] *See* 18 U.S.C. § 922(o) (2011) ("[I]t shall be unlawful for any person to transfer or *possess* a machinegun.") (emphasis added). However, possession may be lawful if the machinegun was lawfully possessed before 1986 and/or subsequently transferred lawfully. *See id.; see also May machineguns be transferred from one registered possessor to another?*, BUREAU OF ALCOHOL, TOBACCO, FIREARMS, AND EXPLOSIVES (last reviewed Sept. 8, 2015), https://atf.gov/firearms/qa/may-machineguns-be-transferred-one-registered-possessor-another (providing guidance on the on lawful machinegun ownership).

possession and use of armed civilian drones in the national airspace. The *No Armed Drones Act of 2017* is a bill to "amend the FAA Modernization and Reform Act of 2012 to establish a prohibition to prevent the use of an unmanned aircraft system as a weapon while in the national airspace[.]"[45] It is a bill that would provide exceptions only for armed drones used in hunting or animal control, and the operations of public UAS, such as those belonging to Customs and Border Control and to the Department of Defense.[46]

While the Act is short, it addresses the problem: it provides a complete and outright ban on these weapons systems from being operated anywhere in the United States. It would enable the FAA, as a component of the Department of Transportation, by vesting in the Secretary the authority to make new rules and regulations regarding the possession of weaponized drones. The only question is whether this is legal or whether Congress would be exceeding its authority with such a broad ban. To determine the legality of this law, it is informative to look at the jurisprudence regarding Federal legislation and the Commerce Clause.

The Commerce Clause empowers Congress with the power to "regulate Commerce . . . among the several States . . . ."[47] In *United States v. Lopez*, the Supreme Court crystallized the degree to which commerce must be involved for a Federal law to be presumptively valid: the basis must arise out of commercial activity before the aggregate activity has a substantial effect that would allow Congress to regulate.[48]

Regarding Federal regulation of safety in civil aviation, it has been grounded in commerce since its beginning.[49] Furthermore, the events of terrorist attacks—and attempted attacks—have been shown to have wide-ranging and severe economic effects.[50] Public safety is also one

---

[45] No Armed Drones Act of 2017, H.R. 129, 115th Cong. (2017).

[46] *Id.* § 2.

[47] U.S. CONST. art. I, § 8, cl. 3.

[48] *See* United States v. Lopez, 514 U.S. 549, 561-63 (1995). The Substantial Effect Standard in *Lopez* was later upheld in United States v. Morrison, 529 U.S. 598 (2000).

[49] *See generally* Aviation and Transportation Security Act, Pub. L. 107-71, 115 Stat. 597 (2001); Federal Aviation Act of 1958, Pub. L. 85-726, 72 Stat. 731 (1958); Civil Aeronautics Act of 1938, Pub. L. 75-706, 52 Stat. 973 (1938); Air Commerce Act of 1926, Pub. L. 69-254, 44 Stat. 568 (1926).

[50] *See generally* Bryan W. Roberts, *The Macroeconomic Impacts of the 9/11 Attack:*

of the stronger governmental interests, and, accordingly, it permits the government to regulate weapons.[51] However, is this enough to intrude on the States' police powers and the Tenth Amendment? Maybe.

The Supreme Court "ordinarily expects a 'clear and manifest' statement from Congress to authorize an unprecedented intrusion into traditional state authority."[52] The *No Armed Drones Act* itself would be a clear and manifest statement from Congress, but since it is modifying a law that arises out of economic activity and treading upon an area traditionally reserved for the States. While the law might be able to be defended, if challenged, it will have to rely on Congress's manifested intent to occupy the field, evidence of the economic effects of terrorism and interstate crime, and the argument of protecting national security from interstate threats in the national airspace, which could only be successfully executed via a Federal regulatory scheme.

III. CONCLUSION

Armed drones pose a severe national security threat that needs to be dealt with on a national scale. As it currently stands, the lack of a uniform ban has resulted in a piecemeal effort by the States has not effectuated a nationwide ban, leaving gaps where the possession of these devices is still permissible. If a prospective terrorist can legally weaponize their drone in one State and then transport it to another to use it, what is stopping them? In fact, what prevents them from using

---

Evidence from Real-Time Forecasting (U.S. DEPARTMENT OF HOMELAND SECURITY, Working Paper August 2009). *See also What Is The Effect Of Terrorism On Global Markets?*, FXCM MARKET INSIGHTS, https://www.fxcm.com/insights/effect-terrorism-global-markets/; John O'Ceallaigh, *London's tourism industry counts cost of latest terrorist attack*, THE TELEGRAPH (Jun. 6, 2017, 6:35 PM); Cynthia Kroet, *Brussels terror attacks cost Belgian economy almost €1 billion: report*, POLITICO (Jul. 26, 2016, 3:40 AM).

[51] *See* Heller v. District of Columbia, 670 F.3d 1244, 1262-64 (2011) (applying intermediate scrutiny and citing District of Columbia v. Heller, 554 U.S. 570 (2008) concerning the government's ability to ban or regulate uncommon weapons).

[52] Rapanos v. United States, 547 U.S. 715, 738 (2006) (referencing BFP v. Resolution Trust Corp., 511 U.S. 531, 544 (1994)).

that legally-armed drone against targets and urban areas in the same State that allowed them to possess such a drone legally?

The only way to ensure that weaponized recreational drones do not become a pervasive threat that law enforcement only can react to and do nothing to prevent is for those drones to be banned under Federal law. The passage of a bill like the *No Armed Drones Act of 2017* is a clear necessity, but one that must be in line with Constitutional Law and our existing Federal system. However, one thing is abundantly clear; we cannot wait until these drones become a weapon of choice for criminals and terrorists.

CRYPTO WARS

By Ryan Johnston*

INTRODUCTION

Encryption and digital communication protections are the cornerstones of protecting individual privacy interests in an era where everything can be shared or divulged with the press of a button. Daniel Richman's article on how the government should tackle encryption follows closely to Deputy Attorney General (DAG) Rosenstein's comments at the 65th Annual Attorney General's Awards.[1] During his remarks, Rosenstein stated that he favors strong encryption but has couched this argument within a caveat that moving towards unbreakable encryption is unreasonable.[2] These remarks run directly counter to what security researchers are saying. Bruce Schneier argued in his piece entitled "Security or Surveillance?" that if we poison all the food at a restaurant we may kill a terrorist, but the harm to the innocent customers will greatly outweigh the positive of catching the terrorist.[3] He further argues that such incidents like the 2014-15 Office of Personnel Management breaches may have been less damaging if the information had been encrypted.

The ease of data theft is correlated with whether the data is encrypted in the first place.[4] If the country moves towards the

---

* *Ryan Johnston is currently a 2019 J.D. candidate at the American University Washington College of Law and the Online Editor of the American University National Security Law Brief.*

[1] *See Cyrus* Farivar, *DOJ: Strong encryption that we don't have access to is "unreasonable"*, ARSTECHNICA (Nov. 9, 2017, 4:25 PM), https://arstechnica.com/tech-policy/2017/11/doj-strong-encryption-that-we-dont-have-access-to-is-unreasonable/ (noting that both Richman and Rosenstein are advocating for governmental access to encryption).
[2] *Id.*
[3] Berkman Ctr., *Don't Panic. Making Progress on the "Going Dark" Debate* 25 (Feb 1, 2016) https://cyber.harvard.edu/pubrelease/dont-panic/Dont_Panic_Making_Progress_on_Going_Dark_Debate.pdf (citing appendix A, Bruce Schneier, *Security or Surveillance?*, 1, 3 (Feb 1, 2016)).
[4] Rick Robinson, *The Impact of a Data Breach can be Minimized Through Encryption*, SECURITY INTELLIGENCE (Oct. 21, 2014), https://securityintelligence.com/the-impact-of-a-data-breach-can-be-minimized-through-encryption/ (arguing that encrypted data that is stolen is useless to thieves).

position that DAG Rosenstein is advocating for the FBI will be able to get at the public's text messages and hard drives, but so will other governments, criminals, and terrorists. We have seen in the past that backdoors built for one purpose are surreptitiously co-opted and used for another.[5] Schneier notes that between June 2004 and March 2005 someone wiretapped more than 100 cell phones belonging to members of the Greek government—the prime minister and the ministers of defense, foreign affairs, and justice—and other prominent Greek citizens.[6] Swedish telecommunications provider Ericsson built this wiretapping capability into Vodafone products but enabled it only for governments that requested it.[7] Greece wasn't one of those governments, but some still-unknown party—a rival political group? organized crime? figured out how to surreptitiously turn the feature "on."[8]

The question here is if the government knows these things are happening globally why do they think that it won't happen domestically? Richman wants to avoid refighting the Crypto Wars;[9] however, his article seems like the opening salvo to rolling back the light touch approach the Obama Whitehouse had taken regarding encryption policy.[10] Richman is quick to note that the DAG didn't call for legislation or regulation but limited his proposal to mass market consumer devices that enable warrant-proof encryption by default.[11]

---

[5] Bruce Schneier, DATA AND GOLIATH: THE HIDDEN BATTLES TO COLLECT YOUR DATA AND CONTROL YOUR WORLD 108 (2015).

[6] *Id.*

[7] *Id.*

[8] *Id.*

[9] Danielle Kehl, Andi Wilson, and Kevin Bankston, *Doomed to Repeat History?: Lessons from the Crypto Wars of the 1990's*, Open Technology Institute at 3-11 (June 2015), https://static.newamerica.org/attachments/3407-doomed-to-repeat-history-lessons-from-the-crypto-wars-of-the-1990s/Crypto%20Wars_ReDo.7cb491837ac541709797bdf868d37f52.pdf (noting the battle between the government and private citizens for access to encrypted communications in the 1990's).

[10] Daniel Richman, *Getting Encryption onto the Front Burner*, LAWFARE (Oct. 26, 2017, 7:00 AM), https://www.lawfareblog.com/getting-encryption-front-burner (stating that encryption regulation was "off the table" during the Obama administration).

[11] *Id.*

The problem with the idea of warrant-proof encryption that there is no such thing.[12] Rosenstein argued that "[o]ur society has never had a system where evidence of criminal wrongdoing was totally impervious to detection, especially when officers obtain a court-authorized warrant."[13] In this case, Rosenstein is right, but the fundamental misunderstanding here is between the collection of data and the understanding of it.[14] If a warrant is obtained, the data can be turned over regardless of whether the government understands it. Encryption does not put users above the law, it simply obfuscates user data from the prying eyes of the government and forces it to spend more time making sense of the information it has collected, rather than barring it from collecting it in the first place.[15] Rosenstein noted "[t]here is a cost to having impregnable security, and we've talked about some of the aspects of that. The cost is that criminals are going to be able to get away with stuff, and that's going to prevent us in law enforcement from holding them accountable."[16] However, this is nothing new, stamping out crime online is an impossible goal. The FBI versus Apple debacle shows that the government has ways to access devices that are locked or encrypted so the argument that we

---

[12] *See* Matt Tait, *Decrypting the Going Dark Debate*, LAWFARE (Oct. 17, 2017), https://www.lawfareblog.com/decrypting-going-dark-debate (noting that going dark has nothing to do with the government's ability to seize a device, and that what the government really means by "warrant-proof" is that they cannot access the data in a device the have seized via a valid warrant).

[13] Richard Chirgwin, *"There has never been a right to absolute privacy" – US Deputy AG slams "Warrant-Proof" crypto*, THE REGISTER (Oct. 11, 2017, 2:16 AM), https://www.theregister.co.uk/2017/10/11/deputy_us_ag_rosenstein_encrypt ion_isnt_free_speech/.

[14] *See* Alfred Ng, *The Myth of Responsible Encryption: Experts Say it Can't Work*, CNET (Oct. 12, 2017), https://www.cnet.com/news/responsible-encryption-deputy-attorney-general-rod-rosenstein-back-doors/.

[15] Kevin Poulsen, *Apple's iPhone Encryption is a Godsend, Even if Cops Hate it*, WIRED (Oct. 8, 2014), https://www.wired.com/2014/10/golden-key/ (arguing that a warrant is a measure of permission for the government to do something they are not normally allowed to do. Having a steel reinforced door does not put your house above a search warrant, it just makes it harder for the police to break in).

[16] Farivar, *supra* note 1.

need to weaken encryption does not hold as much weight as it could absent these avenues.[17]

I. CHOICE OF LAW ISSUES

In addition to the domestic issues weakening encryption would raise, there are examples of foreign states demanding tech companies provide them with access to data stored on devices made by U.S. based tech companies.[18] However, just stating that foreign governments are trying to force domestic tech firms to allow them into devices does not mean those firms will have to turn over the data. Cases like *Yahoo!, Inc. v. La Ligue Contre le Racisme et l'Antisémitisme*[19] have stated that a foreign state may not regulate constitutionally protected speech in the United States by claiming that such speech violates the law of the foreign state.[20] Also, the court in *Bernstein v. U.S. Dep't. of Justice*[21] held that code constitutes speech and is therefore protected under the First Amendment.[22] Any argument that a foreign government could force a domestic company to turn over data, encryption keys or backdoors falls flat since there is jurisprudence that states governments cannot enforce court orders or legislation that would violate the U.S. Constitution.[23] This could be an incentive for countries that do not have multilateral legal assistance treaty (MLAT) with the United States to pursue obtaining one, and for those countries that already have an MLAT to use of it.[24] The argument

---

[17] Amie Stepanovich and Michael Kranicolas, *Why an Encryption Backdoor for Just the "Good Guys" Won't Work*, Just Security (March 2, 2018), https://www.justsecurity.org/53316/criminalize-security-criminals-secure/ (noting that government has techniques to bypass encryption technology and that if they use them on a regular basis law enforcement's fear of people "going dark" is overblown).

[18] Richman, *supra* note 5.

[19] 433 F. 3d 1199 (9th Cir. 2006).

[20] *Id.* at 1213.

[21] 922 F. Supp. 1426 (N.D. Cal. 1996).

[22] *Id.* at 1434 (noting, "[t]he paper, an academic writing explaining plaintiff's scientific work in the field of cryptography, is speech of the most protected kind.")

[23] See *generally*, Yahoo!, Inc. v. La Ligue contre le Racisme et l'Antisémitisme, 433 F. 3d 1199 (9th Cir. 2006).

[24] ACCESS, MUTUAL LEGAL ASSISTANCE TREATIES FAQ, *available at* https://www.mlat.info/faq.

could be made that while MLATs are not the fastest way to procure the information, they do make sure that United States companies or citizens do not have their constitutional rights infringed.

II. THE POTENTIAL RISKS OF COOPERATING WITH THE PRIVATE SECTOR

One direction that the U.S. government can turn for vulnerability exploitation and data recovery is to the private sector. There is already a private market for hackers, and there is concern that the demands of federal, state, and local authorities for access to devices will become unsustainable.[25] The FBI has attempted to unlock 14,000 devices in 2017 succeeding on half of its attempts.[26] It is unclear whether or not the FBI is using outside contractors to access encrypted data, but third-party device hacking could be an avenue perused by law enforcement to lessen the load of devices it has to crack. A potential issue with the use of a third party contractor is whether the use of contractors could lead to national security concerns regarding the leaking of tools used by the FBI, NSA, or CIA to access encrypted data, or if the contractors would have the rights to sell any of the vulnerabilities they find to the companies manufacturing the devices, or to potentially malicious actors. These issues are not unfounded since the government has been wracked with contractor issues, as evidenced by the 2015 theft of the NSA hacking tools by Russian hackers, the Snowden revelations, and the Harold T. Martin III incident.[27] However, if an exploit that the government uses to break into devices is fell into the hands of legitimate security researchers or malicious actors, that would place it into the private sector faster and allow the companies that manufacture such devices to propagate patches that improve overall security in general.

---

[25] Richman, *supra* note 5.

[26] *See* Mallory Locklear, *FBI tried and failed to unlock 7,000 encrypted devices*, ENGADGET (Oct. 23, 2017), https://www.engadget.com/2017/10/23/fbi-failed-unlock-7-000-encrypted-devices/.

[27] Ryan Johnston, *Kaspersky, the NSA, and Data Breaches: Bad Security Practices*, AMERICAN UNIVERSITY NATIONAL SECURITY LAW BRIEF (last modified Nov. 13, 2017, 12:52 PM), http://nationalsecuritylawbrief.com/2017/11/05/kaspersky-nsa-data-breaches-bad-security-practices (explaining that all of these incidents occurred because of poor security measures put in place by the NSA to prevent hackers, or rouge contractors from exfiltrating large amounts of classified data and hacking tools).

III. THE POTENTIAL FOR GOVERNMENT ABUSE VERSUS THE BENEFITS OF GOVERNMENT CONTROL

Richman's concern that government hacking and the accompanying opacity will probably never become the investigatory standard, especially given the newest version of the Vulnerabilities Equity Process (VEP).[28] Many of the changes included in the newest iteration of the VEP do seem to lend themselves to transparency that was not previously seen in previous versions of the VEP.[29] The current VEP tries to consider the difficulties of patching certain systems and the need for swift action when vulnerabilities the government has previously retained are exploited.[30] The new policy also mandates yearly reports about the VEP's operation, including an unclassified summary.[31] While it is too early to tell how much of an impact these new policies will have, they are a step in the right direction. The new iteration of the VEP lends itself to opening the dialogue between private citizens concerned about what the government can do regarding the exploitation of security vulnerabilities, and the government who may need to exploit these security vulnerabilities in order to gather intelligence, evidence, or other materials in order to maintain national security and police the country.

The debate on encryption policy is nothing new, the 1990s saw not only the United States' government, but other industrialized countries

---

[28] Andrew Crocker, *Time Will Tell if the new Vulnerabilities Equities Process is a Step Froward for Transparency*, ELECTRONIC FRONTIER FOUNDATION (Nov. 16, 2017), https://www.eff.org/deeplinks/2017/11/time-will-tell-if-new-vulnerabilities-equities-process-step-forward-transparency; *See also* Vulnerabilities Equity Process of the United States Government Released Nov. 15, 2017, *available at* https://www.whitehouse.gov/sites/whitehouse.gov/files/images/External%20-%20Unclassified%20VEP%20Charter%20FINAL.PDF.

[29] *See generally* THE ELECTRONIC FRONTIER FOUNDATION, VULNERABILITIES EQUITY PROCESS, *available at* https://www.eff.org/files/2016/01/18/37-3_vep_2016.pdf (noting there is no clause in this version of the VEP that at all outlines the partnership of the government with the private sector to share vulnerability data).

[30] *Id.*

[31] *Id.*

advocate for the weakening of communications encryption.[32] They claimed—very similarly to present arguments—that widespread encryption is disastrous to law enforcement.[33] Based on this claim, the U.S. government proposed the "Clipper Chip" which was a device that contained a government master key that would enable the government access to encrypted communications.[34] Most of the push for the Clipper Chip as well as key escrow systems were abandoned in 2000 due to pressure from the emerging internet industry and resistance from American allies.[35]

Currently, firms that provide end-to-end encryption services are moving away from the public-private key system because if a user's private key is compromised the entirety of their communications are compromised.[36] With current technology, keys are not discarded after each transaction.[37] This provides more secure communications but does not allow for holding keys that can be captured and used to decrypt communications.[38] Furthermore, there are authentication

---

[32] Andrea Peterson, *The 'Crypto Wars' of the 1990s are Brewing Again in Washington*, THE WASHINGTON POST (Sept. 10, 2015), https://www.washingtonpost.com/news/the-switch/wp/2015/09/10/the-crypto-wars-of-the-1990s-are-brewing-again-in-washington/?utm_term=.fe25be2108b1.

[33] Nicole Perlroth, *Security Experts Oppose government Access to Encrypted Communications*, THE NEW YORK TIMES (July 7, 2015), https://www.nytimes.com/2015/07/08/technology/code-specialists-oppose-us-and-british-government-access-to-encrypted-communication.html.

[34] Harold Abelson et al., *Keys under doormats: mandating insecurity by requiring government access to all data and communications*, 1 J. OF CYBERSECURITY 69, 71 (2015), https://doi.org/10.1093/cybsec/tyv009.

[35] *Id.* (noting that key escrow is an arrangement in which the keys to decrypt encrypted data are held in escrow so that, under circumstances, an authorized third party may gain access to those keys).

[36] Aaron Reffett, *Implications and Mitigation Strategies for the Loss of End-Entity Private Keys*, SEI Blog (March 19, 2018), https://insights.sei.cmu.edu/sei_blog/2018/03/implications-and-mitigation-strategies-for-the-loss-of-end-entity-private-keys.html (explaining that if a private key is lost the compromised end user can be impersonated, have their received communications decrypted, and or expose other sensitive information).

[37] Scott Helme, *Perfect Forward Secrecy – An Introduction*, SCOTTHELME.CO.UK (May 10, 2014), https://scotthelme.co.uk/perfect-forward-secrecy/.

[38] *Id.*

concerns to giving up keys for encrypted messages.[39] The disclosure of an encryption key doesn't just mean that a party can read the encrypted messages, but it also gives them the ability to fabricate traffic that appears to have come from the original sender.[40] This could give the government unprecedented power to modify what private citizens send and receive, but the more pressing concern would be with what could happen if a malicious third-party accessed the stored keys.

Hopefully, there would be some policy measure in place to keep the government from tampering with an individual's communications, but there could be no such measures in place to prevent a malicious actor from doing the same. One of the most difficult questions we must ask ourselves encompasses all the prior concerns: who would control the keys if some form of mandatory key escrow was put into place? In the United States, it could be assumed that the NSA or FBI would control the keys. As an alternative, a process much like how foreign intelligence data is controlled could also be used. However, there would need to be some system devised so that state and local law enforcement could access the data as well.

Another overarching question centers around what would happen when we try to regulate public and private entities outside the United States. Would other countries be willing to give the U.S. government access to their data, especially if they have a law in place that restricts their government from doing the same? There are many facets to this argument that need to be analyzed before any attempt to implement some form of exceptional access.

People may not realize that other issues also arise as a result of authorizing some form of exceptional access, such as the sheer number of people needed to enforce these policies. There would be engineers that would need to work with both the government and private sector companies to devise the tools that would be used, and

---

[39] Tom Spring, *Hackers Take Aim at SSH Keys in New Attacks*, THREAT POST (Oct. 19, 2017), https://threatpost.com/hackers-take-aim-at-ssh-keys-in-new-attacks/128537/ (discussing how the theft of a private key could give a threat actor access to any server or system where that private key is used for authentication).

[40] Margaret Rouse, *Asymmetric Cryptography (Public Key Cryptography)*, TECHTARGET (last updated June 2016), http://searchsecurity.techtarget.com/definition/asymmetric-cryptography.

lawyers on both sides to debate the legality of any request to gain access to a private citizen's phone.[41] There would also need to be those that write and enforce policies for setting these types of systems and those that manage the systems that have been put in place. Also, the introduction of so many people accessing a server holding information on how to access encrypted consumer devices could introduce the possibility of human error, malicious acts, or some mixture of both. The argument could be made that these problems could be diminished by adequate vetting of anyone working with this information, but public confidence in this would likely be low, as the government has clearly and repeatedly failed to adequately vet its contractors in the past.[42] We also must ask ourselves how the company devising such software will store it. When the issue of the government's use of that software inevitably goes to court, will a defendant or plaintiff's attorney be allowed access to the software to make their case? The sheer number of moving parts involved almost guarantees that the code will leak, putting those whose data is stored by that software at risk.[43] If the government undermines the American people's faith in the technology that we use every day it will only deter them from using that technology, thus producing effects directly counter to the government's intentions. Criminals will know that they can't trust their technology, and they will develop other ways to communicate, thus leaving only law-abiding tech users susceptible to the government's all-seeing eye.

---

[41] Susan Landau, *Punching the Wrong Bag: The Deputy AG Enters the Crypto Wars*, LAWFARE (Oct. 27, 2017, 7:00 AM), https://www.lawfareblog.com/punching-wrong-bag-deputy-ag-enters-crypto-wars.

[42] *See, e.g.* Byron Acohido and Peter Eisler, *Snowden Case: How Low-Level Insider Could Steal From NSA*, USA TODAY (June 11, 2013), https://www.usatoday.com/story/news/nation/2013/06/11/snowden-nsa-hacking-privileged-accounts/2412507/; Tal Kopan, Evan Perez and Laura Jarrett, *Former NSA Contractor Indicted in Stolen Data Case*, CNN (Feb. 8, 2017), https://www.cnn.com/2017/02/08/politics/nsa-contractor-alleged-classified-theft-harold-martin-indictment/index.html; Gordon Lubold and Shane Harris, *Russian Hackers Stole NSA Data on U.S. Cyber Defense*, THE WALL STREET JOURNAL (Oct. 5, 2017), https://www.wsj.com/articles/russian-hackers-stole-nsa-data-on-u-s-cyber-defense-1507222108.

[43] *Id.*

IV. CONCLUSION

Deputy Attorney General Rosenstein's comments seem to paint device manufacturers like Apple and Microsoft as enemies, which is counterproductive if the DOJ wants them as allies in the fight against crime. These companies are often legally required to respond to government requests for information and do so as often as they feel they can. The backtracking and stepping away from the goal of cooperation that Richman seems to hint at fails to recognize that the organization(s) that may need to adapt and change in this situation are not the tech firms, but the FBI. The FBI has long taken a stance on cracking down on communications protections. As technology moves forward so must law enforcement, if the DOJ and FBI want to secure the United States, the way to do that is not force device manufacturers to decrease consumer security protections. Daniel Richman's conclusion that moral panic brings about the enacting of long-overdue policies is misguided; often after a national crisis, legislation is rushed through and leaves a lot to be desired. In this case, mandating that tech firms decrease consumer security protections only seeks to benefit an antiquated way of law enforcement and exposes not only the American people but anyone who owns a device sold in America to far greater risk than they would otherwise see. The crypto-wars are reigniting, but the way forward is not to harm consumers for a nonexistent "greater good."

THE SPIRIT OF NORTH AMERICANISM FOR SECURITY AND DIPLOMACY: A CASE STUDY OF THE U.S.–MEXICO BORDER

By Irving Vidal Terrazas*

INTRODUCTION

Over the first two years of the U.S. President Trump administration, the long-lasting, stable relationship between Mexico and the United States (U.S.) has changed dramatically. The new U.S. presidential administration has brought into question many of the latent issues affecting both nations, including security, immigration, economic growth, and the divergence of strategies. The changes directly affect the U.S.–Mexico border's dynamics regarding how both countries' people interact, how policies are created, and how ideas about justice and security develop and evolve. Though billions of dollars are invested to protect the U.S.–Mexico border from transnational crime and terrorism, this still proves a deficient effort to stop weapons smuggling, drug trafficking, and human smuggling. This essay focuses on the potential threats to security and law enforcement in the context of the border region.

I. BACKGROUND

Historically, the two nations have cooperated to prevent incidents along the border through initiatives such as the *Border Violence Prevention Protocols.*[1] These protocols incorporate the exchange of information between authorities from both nations. Even though simulations and meetings occur regularly, mutual distrust prevents information from flowing between U.S. and

---

* *Irving Vidal Terrazas is a LL.M. ILSP 2018 graduate of American University's Washington College of Law, alumnus of the American University National Security Law Brief, and former Director General of the National Central Bureau of INTERPOL Mexico.*

[1] DEPARTMENT OF HOMELAND SECURITY, U.S.–MEXICO 21ST CENTURY BORDER INITIATIVE PROPOSED 2013 ACTION ITEMS, https://www.dhs.gov/sites/default/files/publications/21cb-2013-action-plan.pdf (providing an overview of proposed items to be incorporated as a part of a cross-border initiative).

Mexican personnel as intended; this shared effort has functioned more reactively rather than preventively.

Another recent strategy during President Obama's administration focused on enhancing coordination of intelligence sharing with Mexico, on the Southwest Border High-Intensity Drug Trafficking Areas (HIDTA), including information provided to and received from Mexican agencies.[2] The U.S government explored a more thorough collaboration, in information analytics and sharing, and other collaborative efforts with Mexico's Center for Investigation and National Security (CISEN) and its other intelligence and law enforcement entities. Nonetheless, this effort had a similar result since the trust continues to be only for reactive operations rather than preventive. Consequently, border security remains fragile for both nations.

Following 9/11, United Nation's Security Council resolution 1373/01 obliged member states to criminalize intentional acts of terrorism. It also called on states to cooperate, particularly through bilateral and multilateral arrangements and agreements, to prevent and suppress terrorist attacks and act against the perpetration of such acts.[3] Cooperation between Mexico and the U.S. has proven to be difficult to formalize, as States have even struggled to even agree on a common definition of terrorism.[4] The adage that "one person's

---

[2] *See* OFFICE OF THE NATIONAL DRUG CONTROL POLICY, NATIONAL SOUTHWEST BORDER COUNTERNARCOTICS STRATEGY, EXECUTIVE OFFICE OF THE PRESIDENT OF THE UNITED STATES OF AMERICA 12 (2011), https://obamawhitehouse.archives.gov/sites/default/files/ondcp/policy-and-research/swb_counternarcotics_strategy11.pdf#page=18 (stating goals concerning how to improve cross-border information sharing and joint analysis as a part of the counternarcotics effort).

[3] *See* S.C. Res. 1373, ¶ 3(c) (Sep. 28, 2001), http://www.un.org/en/ga/search/view_doc.asp?symbol=S/RES/1373%20%282001%29 (condemning the terrorist attacks of September 11, 2001, and directs member States to criminalize acts of terrorism, freeze the economic assets of persons who commit acts of terror, and refrain from providing support or safe haven to terrorists).

[4] LORD CARLILE OF BERRIEW Q.C., THE DEFINITION OF TERRORISM 3 (2007), https://assets.publishing.service.gov.uk/government/uploads/system/upload s/attachment_data/file/228856/7052.pdf (concluding that, based on exhaustive research of various definitions provided in international and

terrorist is another person's freedom fighter" reflects more of a political than a legal or semantic challenge to achieving the UN's goal.[5] Fortunately, and despite the differences between the U.S. and Mexican legal systems, both nations have reached a sense of legal middle ground. Hence, this would not be the first time that these two nations endeavor to address different matters of international cooperation based on a treaty. Although lately questioned by the current U.S. presidential administration, the most concrete and ambitious project of regional multilateralism (with Canada) was NAFTA, a comprehensive free trade and investment treaty linking the economic fortunes of party nations.[6]

II. ANALYSIS

In spite of the simple, if politically inflammatory, decision to build a fence or wall that would deter and prevent smuggling people, drugs, and weapons, their crossing continues between the two countries. Reinforcing such policy by actually building a wall will only result in further political alienation, rather than a solution.

A. Unsuccessful strategies

Over the past decade, the threats to North America's security have grown significantly. The U.S.–Mexican border has proven unable to stop drugs crossing to the United States, while also failing to stop weapons from crossing into Mexico. From late 2009 to early 2011, as a part of Operation Fast and Furious, the Phoenix Field Division of the Bureau of Alcohol, Tobacco, Firearms, and Explosives allowed the illegal gun sales of nearly 2,000 firearms with the intent to track the sellers and buyers, believed to be part of Mexican drug cartels.[7]

---

foreign legal systems, "[t]here is no universally accepted definition of terrorism.")

[5] PHILIP ALSTON & RYAN GOODMAN, INTERNATIONAL HUMAN RIGHTS 383 (2012).

[6] SHANNON K. O'NEIL, TWO NATIONS INDIVISIBLE: THE UNITED STATES, AND THE ROAD AHEAD 25 (2013).

[7] KELLY COHEN, *Justice Department to turn over 'Fast and Furious' documents to House panel*, Washington Examiner (Mar. 07, 2018, 1:15 PM), https://www.washingtonexaminer.com/justice-department-to-turn-over-fast-and-furious-documents-to-house-panel/article/2650939 (providing a

Unfortunately, not all aspects of this operation went well for the U.S. government.[8] On the night of December 14, 2010, a U.S. Border Patrol Tactical Unit (BORTAC) confronted an armed group in Peck Canyon, Rio Rico, Arizona,[9] about 25 miles north of Nogales.[10] As a result of the firefight, a single bullet reached Agent Brian Terry.[11] According to his fellow agents at the shooting, the Border Patrol Agent lost consciousness and died while he was taken to the hospital after midnight.[12] After tracing the two AK-47 assault rifles recovered at the scene, it was found that they were part of Operation Fast and Furious.[13] A straw purchaser with known connections to the Mexican drug cartels had purchased the firearms from a shop in Glendale, Arizona on January 16, 2010.[14] Allegations the Mexican government knew about this operation fueled feelings of mistrust among the public, and more importantly, the failures of this

---

brief description of the operation as a part of the context for an article about the settling of litigation brought by the House Oversight and Government Reform Committee against then-Attorney General Eric Holder for the release of documents concerning the botched operation).

[8] *See* Sara Horwitz, *Operation Fast and Furious: A gunrunning sting gone wrong,* THE WASHINGTON POST (Jul. 26, 2011), https://www.washingtonpost.com/investigations/us-anti-gunrunning-effort-turns-fatally-wrong/2011/07/14/gIQAH5d6YI story.html?noredirect=on&utm term=.207a 565caa52 (describing the plan behind the operation and subsequently how the operation's failures came to be seen as the Bureau of Arms, Tobacco, Firearms, and Explosives' biggest debacle since the 1993 Waco incident).

[9] Devin Dwyer, *Agent Brian Terry Shot in Back with AK-47 During Gunfight, Family Says,* ABC NEWS (Dec. 15, 2010), https://abcnews.go.com/US/border-patrol-agent-shot-killed-us-mexico-border/story?id=12401948.

[10] UNITED STATES CONGRESS, 115TH CONGRESS, JOINT STAFF REP., FAST AND FURIOUS: OBSTRUCTION OF CONGRESS BY DEPARTMENT OF JUSTICE, PART III 5 (2017), https://oversight.house.gov/wp-content/uploads/2017/06/FINAL REPORT 2017.pdf#page=5.

[11] *Id.*

[12] *Id.*

[13] *Id.* at 6.

[14] *Id.*

operation highlighted the importance of trust in the proper channels of intelligence sharing.[15]

The U.S. has taken a step forward by decriminalizing and legalizing marijuana, which has been the vehicle for cash flow to the cartels while smuggling stronger and more profitable drugs. Although the U.S government has funded the intelligence resources for counter narcotics, the primary goal has been to stop the drugs crossing and strengthening law enforcement.[16] The issue then becomes, whether the allocation of the funds is based on an equivocal strategy or if such funds should be placed in other efforts such as a binational intelligence core.

President Donald Trump set two cornerstones during his 2016 campaign; immigration and border security. Following his inauguration, he "signed executive orders calling for the construction of a border wall between the two countries and increases in border patrol personnel."[17] Tensions between the United States and Mexico could easily increase as a result of the Trump Administration's policies, and this has some experts worried that cooperation on security policy will be negatively affected.[18]

The Mexican government had to modify its strategy in order accomplish reducing the activity of the drug cartels from a national security issue to a law enforcement problem by addressing the matter with the military forces' intervention and to subsequently allocate the duty again to the police.[19] Numerous policymakers and U.S. government officers have expressed their concerns in regards to the Mexican authority's capabilities to reduce the violence in the country and reduce the

---

[15] *See AP Exclusive: Second Bush-Era Gun-Smuggling Probe*, ASSOCIATED PRESS, Oct. 14, 2011, http://www.foxnews.com/us/2011/10/14/ap-exclusive-second-bush-era-gun-smuggling-probe.html.

[16] Brianna Lee & Danielle Renwick, *Mexico's Drug War*, COUNCIL ON FOREIGN RELATIONS (last updated May 25, 2017), https://www.cfr.org/backgrounder/mexicos-drug-war.

[17] *Id.*

[18] *Id.*

[19] June S. Beittel, CONG. RESEARCH SERV., R41476, MEXICO: ORGANIZED CRIME AND DRUG TRAFFICKING ORGANIZATIONS 28 (2017), https://fas.org/sgp/crs/row/R41576.pdf#page=31.

influence of the Mexican Cartels.[20] President Peña- Nieto's strategy on targeting the main drug cartel leaders offers no sustainable solution, regardless of temporary reducing the violence in some regions. For some observers, Mexico's drug cartels challenge remains largely an organized crime or mafia problem, coupled with endemic corruption.[21]

B. Latent threats

While the primary focus of vulnerabilities is drug cartels, the presence of other radical organizations such as Hezbollah and Iran's Qods Force in Latin America has become a more imminent threat to the security of North America.[22] In August 2012, a U.S. congressional delegation visited Argentina, Mexico, Colombia and other countries to confer with foreign leaders and other experts within these countries on hemispheric security.[23] The delegation concluded that Iran and Hezbollah pose a threat to the entire Western Hemisphere, highlighting the U.S. southern border with Mexico.[24]

These latent threats to security become an even greater challenge when considering the effective regional and global approach taken by criminal and terrorist organizations. Some illicit organizations have tapped into a vast network through the Mexican drug cartels to finance terrorists and other illicit activities in the Middle East and South America.[25] The nexus of these cartels has reached even the attempted assassination of a foreign dignitary in the U.S.[26]

---

[20] *Id.*

[21] *Id.*

[22] *See* Michael T. McCaul, H. COMM. ON HOMELAND SEC., SUBCOMMITTEE ON OVERSIGHT, INVESTIGATIONS AND MANAGEMENT, 112TH CONG. MAJORITY REP., A LINE IN THE SAND: COUNTERING CRIME, VIOLENCE AND TERROR AT THE SOUTHWEST BORDER 7-10 (2012), https://homeland.house.gov/files/11-15-12-Line-in-the-Sand.pdf#page=9.

[23] *Id.* at 7.

[24] *Id.*

[25] *See id.* at 14-15.

[26] *See* Press Release, Department of Justice, Manssor Arbabsiar Sentenced in New York City Federal Court to 25 Years in Prison for Conspiring with Iranian Military Officials to Assassinate the Saudi Arabian Ambassador to the United States (May 30, 2013), https://www.justice.gov/opa/pr/manssor-arbabsiar-sentenced-new-york-city-federal-court-25-years-prison-

Another incident that stunned the Intelligence community was a car bomb detonated by the drug cartels in Ciudad Juarez in 2010, less than 2 miles from the border with El Paso, Texas.[27] According to Mexican and U.S. investigation teams, the perpetrators placed into the vehicle parked on the curb, up to 22 pounds of a water gel explosive called Tovex, which is used commonly as a substitution for dynamite in mining.[28] Shortly after the attack occurred, the ambassadors from both nations proffered their remarks by differentiating the incident from terrorist acts. In fact, the U.S. ambassador referred to terrorism as being "acts by groups with political objectives that seek to control the government."[29] However, the Mexican Ambassador indicated that "[w]hat is important is not to create the perception that it was an indiscriminate act against civilians. It was not placed in the middle of a market. It was clearly directed against the police."[30] This incident highlights how existing latent threats and capabilities of the drug cartels can be activated at any time.

Some argue drug cartels are at the point of being considered terrorist organizations. In 2011, the U.S. Representative Michael McCaul, the chairman of the Homeland Security Oversight and Investigations Subcommittee, introduced a bill that would add Mexico's six dominant cartels—the Arellano Felix organization, Los Zetas, Beltran Leyva, Familia Michoacana, Sinaloa Cartel, and the Gulf Cartel, Jalisco New Generation—to the State Department's

---

conspiring-iranian (announcing the sentence of Manssor Arbabsiar for his role in the attempted assassination of the Saudi Arabian ambassador to the United States, and detailing his part in the planning and coordination, including his attempt to go through a representative of a Mexican drug cartel).

[27] William Booth, *Ciudad Juarez car bomb shows new sophistication in Mexican drug cartels' tactics*, THE WASHINGTON POST (Jul. 22, 2010), http://washingtonpost.com/wp-dyn/content/article/2010/07/21/AR2010072106200.html?sid=ST2010072106244.

[28] *Id.*

[29] *Id.*

[30] *Id* at ¶ 2.

foreign terrorist organizations list.[31]   However, the Mexican government has constantly stated that, regardless of the unprecedented level of violence, drug cartels are not terrorist organizations nor they are seeking a political agenda to destabilize the government.[32] Cartels do not hate a particular group other than their rivals to whom they attack with unparalleled brutality.[33]

Some of the tactics are used by the cartels to instill fear among the population, at the same time that it goes back and forth with the government. This includes the most recent video spread on social networks in which, like the Islamic State (ISIS), presents its captives to express a specific message and purpose.[34] Pressed in front of the cameras and with hands behind their backs, two missing agents, revealed information that further empowered the cartel during the administration of President Enrique Peña.[35]   The adoption of insurgent and terrorist techniques by organized crime groups in Mexico, which is reflected in the use of car bombs, grenades, and grenade launchers during their attacks, is a situation of concern to the U.S. Congress.[36] The constant use of car bombs, grenades, and rocket-propelled grenade launchers continues to raise concerns that

---

[31] Rafael Romo, *Mexican drug cartels considered terrorist?*, CNN (Apr. 15, 2011, 2:49   PM), http://www.cnn.com/2011/WORLD/americas/04/15/cartels.terror/index.html.
[32] *Id.* It is also worth noting Mexican Ambassador to the United States Arturo Sarukhan's response to support expressed by the newspaper the Dallas Morning News for Representative McCaul's bill. The Ambassador responded in a letter to the editor, saying that "if you label [drug cartels] as terrorist [organizations], you will have to start calling drug consumers in the U.S. 'financiers of terrorist organizations' and gun dealers 'providers of material support to terrorists.' Otherwise, … you really sound as if you want to have your cake and eat it too." *Id.*
[33] *Id.* Mexican authorities also insist that the only true motive of the cartels is cash. *Id.*
[34] Gardenia Mendoza, *¿Imita cártel Jalisco Nueva Generación tácticas terroristas?* [*Does the Jalisco Cartel New Generation mimic terrorist tactics?*], LA OPINIÓN, (Feb. 12, 2018), https://laopinion.com/2018/02/12/imita-cartel-jalisco-nueva-generacion-tacticas-terroristas/.
[35] *Id.*
[36] Beittel, *supra* note 20, at 4.

some Mexican drug cartels may be adopting insurgent or terrorist techniques.[37]

More recently, even the U.S. authorities have expressed their concern in this regard stating that Mexican drug cartels are linked with ISIS and other criminal organizations.[38] In fact, the criminal cartels have refined their technological and operational tactics. The cartels hire hitmen with combat abilities equivalent to military forces.[39] Sophistication and global reach create a complex law enforcement problem, even threatening national security through contacts and potential to cooperate with terrorist organizations.[40]

III. RECOMMENDATION

In recognition of the tensions that divide the U.S. and Mexico and the challenges that unite them, the creation of a new bilateral intelligence core treaty is necessary. At the heart of this treaty is the creation of an intelligence core within a binational law enforcement body that distributes investments and responsibilities for security equally between the two states.

The proposed treaty is to include a formal channel of intelligence exchange creating the necessary reliability on the information gathered and shared. By formalizing a treaty for this specific purpose, Washington, D.C. and Mexico City will be responsible for addressing common issues targeting the specific objectives and for avoiding unstable solutions.

---

[37] Ana Langner, *Preocupa a EU técnicas terroristas de cartels* [*US concerns about terrorist cartel techniques*], EL ECONOMISTA (Aug. 2, 2017, 10:36 PM), https://www.eleconomista.com.mx/politica/Preocupa-a-EU-tecnicas-terroristas-de-carteles-20170803-0083.html.

[38] Elena Toledo, *US Government confirms connection between Mexican Drug Cartels and ISIS*, PANAM POST (Jun. 18, 2017), https://panampost.com/elena-toledo/2017/06/15/us-government-confirms-connection-between-mexican-drug-cartels-and-isis/ (citing then-Secretary of State Rex Tillerson's concerns about connections between the cartels and ISIS, and he implied that disruption those connections "is part of our global effort to deny funding to terrorists").

[39] *When organized crime connects to international terror*, TIME RECORD NEWS (Jun. 28, 2017, 2:16 PM CT), https://www.timesrecordnews.com/story/opinion/2017/06/28/when-organized-crime-connects-international-terror/436660001/.

[40] *Id.*

Furthermore, this could be a great opportunity to envision a new agreement related to addressing issues that have not been openly addressed. The agreement will also involve the undertaking of necessary measures to address the widespread corruption within Mexico. This is a critical moment in history in which both nations must acknowledge the issues and take an effective joint forward effort to address them.

With the proposed treaty, the binational intelligence core and law enforcement operations will be strengthened by simplifying the bureaucracy for extradition proceedings, mutual legal assistance, and prosecution, regardless of both U.S. and Mexico's different legal systems. This strategy will result in reducing costs significantly for both countries and increasing the rights protection of the individuals involved. As an example, the availability of a list of the most wanted fugitives for both nations can reduce the efforts by focusing on the defined priorities and specific individuals. This system has been proven to work globally for close to a century with INTERPOL's red notice.

IV. CONCLUSION

It is time for both nations to leave the blame game off of the negotiation table. It has been proved that it diminishes the capacity to address the issues thoroughly. The allocation of funds should be focused on being effective rather than reactive for intelligence and law enforcement. The U.S. and Mexico's attempts individually to diminish or solve the issues have been unsuccessful since drugs, money, and weapons continue crossing the border, which increases violence. The proposed treaty will provide another feasible alternative instead of reinforcing the failed policies. This is an option that should be explored since, Mexico pursued a comprehensive public diplomacy strategy to rebrand Mexico in the minds of Americans from 1989 to 1994 and from 2000 to 2002 despite the limitations of history, power asymmetry, and interdependence.[41] As challenging as it seems, and acknowledging the interdependence

---

[41] Pamela Karr, *Mexican Public Diplomacy: Hobbled by History, Interdependence and Asymmetric Power*, PUBLIC DIPLOMACY MAGAZINE (Jun. 1, 2010), http://www.publicdiplomacymagazine.com/mexican-public-diplomacy-hobbled-by-history-interdependence-and-asymmetric-power/.

between U.S. and Mexico, this is an innovative approach to explore a formal agreement.

A treaty or covenant will incite a commitment from both nations, instead of leaving it just to politics. Certainly, this proposal can address the security issues together to eradicate the vulnerability. Integration in North America between these two countries and their symbiosis has been part of their history. As Ronald Reagan expressed in November 1979 with his visionary perspective, "[t]he key to our own future security may lie in both Mexico and Canada becoming much stronger countries than they are today... it is time we stopped thinking of our nearest neighbors as foreigners . . . ."[42] The United States and Mexico need to rise up again with the spirit of North Americanism[43] to attend to one of the most challenging moments in their history, in which a strong, direct, and informed diplomacy will be the protagonist.

---

[42] KIRON K. SKINNER ET AL., REAGAN: A LIFE IN LETTERS 509 (2004).
[43] ROBERT A PASTOR, THE NORTH AMERICAN IDEA: A VISION OF A CONTINENTAL FUTURE loc. 3161-3164 (2011) (ebook).

www.ingramcontent.com/pod-product-compliance
Lightning Source LLC
Chambersburg PA
CBHW072205170526
45158CB00004BB/1774